Interactive Christianity

Connecting the Dots:
The interactions of Christ followers
that result in making disciples.

John W. Mowat

authorHOUSE

AuthorHouse™
1663 Liberty Drive
Bloomington, IN 47403
www.authorhouse.com
Phone: 833-262-8899

Published by AuthorHouse 01/06/2021

ISBN: 978-1-6655-1222-0 (sc)
ISBN: 978-1-6655-1221-3 (e)

Library of Congress Control Number: 2020925878

Contents

Introduction

Yes

It is possible! **You** can be effectively involved in influencing those around you to respond to God's love and discover who He is as they come to know Jesus Christ in a personal way. This can be done using the unique gifts, personality, and talent God has given you. It can be done right where you are, in your present or future circumstance, without being rude, or in appropriately forcing yourself, or forcing something else on those around you. Jesus Christ was forceful especially with proud hypocritical people, His word is sharp as a double edge sword, yet He was gentle, especially with lost, hurting, needy people. You can be too.

This book is written for a variety of persons in all stages of Christian development. **It is written first and foremost for those who want to share their faith** but don't have specialized speaking skills and talents, and don't know how to do so without being offensive.

It is written especially for Pastors who are seeking to understand how God desires to use the people who associate with their local church to reach lost people in their community. This book looks at the full range of interactions necessary in both the church and individuals, Interactions that are essential to the whole task of making disciples.

If pastors understand these interactions, see them as central to Christ's mission, see them as an integral aspect of every area of Christian living; if the interactions described here then become a pastor's priority, these pastors can have a unique influence in assisting other Christians in both their knowledge and experience of Christ, as he lives in us and through us. As ongoing students of the word, of life, and of people, these <u>pastors can and must give practical application far beyond what is contained here.</u>

Next it is written *for all of those who are in fact serious about following and obeying Christ,* especially as it relates to their own God given ministry. It is written to help people to understand and discover that without being a specialist, I.E. pastor, evangelist, etc. they can have a ministry that is equally important, if not sometimes more important than a specialist.

Among those Christ followers who work and live in the everyday world there is the widest possible diversity, this diversity includes the types of gift or talent; interest level, personality type, or stage of development in their walk with Christ. This diversity will tend to match the diversity of the community in which they live thus the opportunity to be leaven wherever God has placed them.

At the outset, however, it is important to be clear.

There are many methods and means of Evangelism. This is especially true of those especially gifted and equipped to in some way be "an evangelist". There are however, far fewer means and methods for those who are not up front leaders with specialized gifts and calling.

It is a grave error however, to believe that because of this, people not called or gifted to be pastors, etc., are less important, perhaps even useless except as a supporting cast for the pastor, to do the work of the ministry within the confines of the local church.

God has uniquely placed each of us. While persons without unique gifts, may be the ones who sit in the pew on Sundays, they are also those whose daily lives normally are, or can be fully enmeshed with the world of unbelievers. As such, non-clergy have a unique advantage in communicating the gospel to those persons God has placed around them. They are already fully immersed in their communities ready to be yeast or leaven to the whole community. Often because of their unique gifts, personality, place in the community, etc. they may be the only person who can touch those individuals with the gospel.

Jesus gives us many different descriptions of what the "kingdom of God" is like. When I look at the basic relationships that the non-clergy have in their day to day lives, and realize the extent to which they are a part of every portion of society, I am brought face to face with Jesus parables of the mustard seed and of yeast. Mustard: start small, grow tall and strong as a tree. Yeast: mixed in till it works through it all. **This is where the lay person have their greatest strength!**

This book **is not** intended to answer the questions as to what programs, what special events, or what community involvements the local church, or the larger organized church should be involved with. Rather it attempts to look first, primarily at the role of the **individual believer** as they will be found at any and every strata of society, with any and every personality type. These believers can, and already do touch unbelievers where they live without the need to force themselves on anyone, or cross difficult barriers. Then, second to look at these same believers as they are a part of the whole church in the process of making disciples.

What I share here is, I believe the _very foundation of all other methods of evangelism,_ because it flows out from our most basic personal relationships. It flows out of our relationship with God Himself, our relationship with other believers, and it flows out of our natural connections and relationship with unbelievers.

Historically virtually every major breakdown in the effectiveness of the church in evangelism, can be traced to a breakdown in one or more of these relationships. It can be traced to a breakdown in the **LOVE RELATIONSHIP;** it can be traced to a breakdown in loving God, and our neighbor, both those who are believers, and especially those who are unbelievers.

Jesus taught us that two commandments summarized all the others. **Love God** with all your heart, soul and strength. **Love your neighbor**, as yourself. Obeying Christ's command to make disciples becomes easy and natural to the extent that we first learn how to love. Any method of evangelism that fails to love, fails in the long run, and tends to be unfruitful and ineffective. Even when we attempt to obey the command to make disciples, if we do not love as commanded, there is a breakdown, and as in I Cor. 13, we become as blaring brass and crashing cymbals.

Learning to love God, learning to love man, is not possible in the manner Jesus taught, **in our own strength.** Even when constantly and repeatedly yielding to the Spirit of God in our life, learning to love is a lifetime learning experience, but without this love we are impotent in communicating the life changing good news Jesus proclaimed.

There are **two distinctive's of this book**: one, the approach to evangelism is **intentionally centered in the World**, in the everyday locations in which we all live. The books primary evangelistic focus is on these personal interactions, rather than centering in activities of the local church. It focuses on every persons **everyday** interactions with unbelievers, rather than with event centered evangelism in which the spot light is on the pastor as evangelist and the laypersons are only the supporting cast. Seen from this perspective the pastoral staff is the supporting cast as they "prepare God's people for works of service" Eph. 4:12. Only when we begin looking at our interactions as believers with each other does this focus change. Even then it is designed to show how we support one another.

Second, I have a strong conviction that in **John 13:31- 17:26 Jesus sets forth his intended method for completing His ministry of reconciliation of the world to Himself.**

IE. John 13:31 – 17:26 is Jesus training manual for World Evangelism.

To sum up:

Jesus method of evangelism is this.

He intends to Himself **indwell** the believer through the Holy Spirit following His return to heaven, and **thus be present** wherever his people are throughout the world and draw people to Himself.

Assuming this to be true, in most churches, even evangelical churches, a radical paradigm shift is required. **A shift is required which sees the whole body of Christ as the real ministers, see their everyday associations in the world of unbeliever's, as their primary and first area of ministry, and see the ministerial Staff (Clergy) as equippers for this ministry.** A DNA shift will be required in which the entire program of the Church shifts to give time and priority to make this possible. All other outreach programs should flow out of these basic interactions with Christ, unbelievers, and other believers.

While God has many and varied ways of spreading the gospel. Many and varied ways that He works through His people, I have come to strongly believe that His first and primary means is through the **person to person** contacts that virtually everyone has.

In part one **The Body of Christ: meant to interact.** I share a theological perspective on the body of Christ, which often pastors believe that they share; which however, their approach to ministry often does not reflect. Pastors, I ask you to look again at the overall focus of your preaching and programs. Look again at the whole of the Scripture, try to understand God's purpose in everything he does and says; His directions to you personally, using your individual gifts and those of your congregation.

This book is not intended as a new formula, rather its intention is to take a fresh look at how God has been, still is, and still does want to work through all of His people, the body of Christ, to reach a lost world and bring all that are willing to Himself.

Try to clearly distinguish between the role of building the outward structure of the church, i.e. the trellis designed to support the vine, or the scaffolding required to build the building, and that of building the Church, adding to the body of Christ itself.

The Body of Christ: meant to interact, is largely a foundational biblical study. In it, I have attempted to establish a clear biblical picture of the Body of Christ, and how Christ wishes to use it to accomplish his mission. This has been placed first in the book because I believe that as we study the Scriptures regarding the Body of Christ, there is a core of truth, which if taken to heart radically changes our approach to ministry and our expectations in fulfilling Christ's mandate.

Part two, **A Christ follower's interaction with Christ,** has been written because this interaction is foundational for every other interaction. Without this foundation of truly dwelling in Christ and He in us, we are as the Scribes and Pharisees who Christ stated made converts to turn them into worse children of the Devil than themselves.

Part three, **A Christ follower's interaction with unbelievers** is the central focus of this book. However, standing alone it is mechanical and worthless. Its intention is to assist us in intelligently approaching the unbeliever with the good news regarding Jesus Christ. Please do not even read it without first a careful reading of part 2 and an honest evaluation of your own relationship with God through Jesus Christ.

Part four, **the Christ follower's interaction with other believers in the process of making Disciples** is focused on areas that the pastor and local church leaders need to prayerfully and carefully consider as they plan the ministries of the Church. This area can be helpful to others in the church and should be considered as they are working with responsive people, but individuals not in leadership have little control of this larger arena.

This writer's and a historical perspective

This book comes from having lived long in both worlds; the world of the pulpit, and the world of the Pew. Having spent nearly half of my career in the pulpit attempting to do, learn, and teach evangelism, I relinquished that role, and took up the role of a businessman in the world of construction. It was in this final phase of my active work life, as I wrestled with God, his word, and people in their normal daily life, that God has taught me in real life, that which I attempt to share in this book.

When I was about 14, struggling to be a follower of Christ, I got a few things straightened out at a Sunday night alter of prayer. Following this I felt impelled to go talk with our neighbors about what I was experiencing. They weren't friends, they weren't even just neighbors; they were the enemy. They shot at our dogs if they strayed out into our pasture anywhere near their line fence. I went. I don't remember anything else, except that the next Sunday night they were in Church. That experience began a lifelong pursuit of both attempting to be used of God to bring others to Him, as well as trying to understand how God wants to work, and how he wants to work through us, to have it happen.

Much has changed in the church landscape in the 60 plus years that I have been a follower of Jesus Christ. When I was young, WWII was a clear memory, television was a new experience. Driving 6 miles to town was a weekly event, wherein you got what you needed or waited until the next week. Much of community life revolved around the church. Evangelical denominations could still get unsaved people to come for special church centered events. Getting people saved was all that mattered. And that generally happened through the pulpit in some manner. Personal evangelism was yet in its infancy. Main line denominations were known among evangelicals for their rejection of the authority and inerrancy of the Word and for their socialization of the gospel.

Throughout the Twentieth century mainline denominations generally lost their constituency, because their message increasingly became irrelevant and meaningless.

Evangelicals generally lost their audience because they both separated themselves from those they considered sinners in order to live a life of righteousness and because the "holiness" they proclaimed, often was seen by the sinner for its hypocrisy. Since outward morality itself can often be attained without the need for church attendance; the world did not feel a need for the church, or need its condemnation. Neither the charitable acts without good news of a changed life, or religion without caring about the daily struggles of life, appealed to the masses. Consequently the Church lost ground in America in most quarters. Obviously this is an oversimplification. However, as we moved through the 60's, 70's, 80's, 90's, and beyond, the church in most quarters continued to lose its relevancy to the world around it.

Resulting from these forces several things have happened across the church world. Main line denominations often have been split and re-split as those who desired to maintain devotion to the word of God, warred with those who wished to make man the judge of what was true and false.

Evangelicals have gone a number of different directions. Many have carried on as if little or nothing had or were happening, content with their own little fellowship. These individual were often in deep seclusion to avoid real or imagined persecution, or persecution not resulting from the cross of Christ, but rather from their culturally religious practice. Many individuals and families have flitted here and there seeking for the best act in town.

The Movement to reach the world outside the church, on a person to person basis has moved through several different phases from the 60's thru the current times. In the late 60's and 70's Personal evangelism was the catch word. You personally were responsible to find some way to catch someone and speak the words of the gospel. Little tools such as the Four Spiritual Laws, developed by Bill Bright and Campus Crusade were the in thing. These tools were effective in speaking the words of the gospel in a concise way. But they were often used without regard for where the target was at, either in their understanding or attitude. At best this often resulted in an intellectual decision with no follow up or discipling process. Many persons in the Church who really wanted to obey Christ's command and who did want to win their friends to Christ were very turned off by these material because it seemed callous and insensitive "to button-hole people" and the results were often embarrassing. Others never attempted because to them it seemed that they could not or were excused from this, because, they did not have the gift.

This approach was followed, on its heels, by materials such as Evangelism Explosion by James Kennedy and the Coral Ridge Presbyterian Church in Florida. These materials had the advantage of a bit more length, allowing more initial understanding and used in the context of the local church, perhaps follow up of new believers and discipling. By the 1980's the church was being exposed to materials then called Lifestyle evangelism. These materials were definitely a step forward, introducing the importance of sharing the gospel in the context of our lifestyle, but with limited understanding of how this might take place. The current catch word, if there is one would be relational evangelism. However there is still little broad understanding in the church as a whole, of this vital relationship that God intends for every believer to have with those whom God has placed around them. Often individuals have an understanding of this relationship, but are not part of a church whose DNA provides an adequate community for nurture and discipling.

In most churches, even evangelical churches, even churches who think they are a equipping church, a radical paradigm shift is required. **A shift is required which sees the whole body of Christ as the real ministers, see their everyday associations in the world of unbeliever's, as their primary and first area of ministry, and see the ministerial Staff**

(Clergy) as equippers for this ministry. A DNA shift will be required in which the entire program of the Church shifts to give time and priority to make this possible. <u>All other outreach programs should flow out of these basic interactions with Christ, unbelievers, and other believers.</u>

Among evangelicals, especially in the ranks of churches that have become known as mega churches, the current emphasis is to be outwardly focused. This obviously attempts to address the past neglect of U S evangelicals to address the social needs of their own communities. It is to be greatly commended and encouraged. *However if it is done in the absence of real love for individuals, in the absence of relating to them personally, with sensitivity to their uniqueness, **and** an ability to speak the words of gospel to that unique person, this outward focus can degenerate into the social gospel of the past century.*

Even among those churches most successful in drawing people through being outwardly focused, I find little that is addressed to meet the need of equipping their people for the ministry of relating to those God places around them in their workplace, their neighborhoods, and their families on a daily basis. Ephesians 4 teaches us that a primary biblical role of pastors and teachers is to equip the body of Christ for <u>its</u> ministry. This book is an attempt to narrow that gap left by generations in which little equipping has taken place. <u>It is also a book attempting to see each of these equipped individual as part of a local church in which it's DNA includes the full orbed relationships that lead to ongoing healthy evangelism.</u>

As a young pastor, I studied and used most of the material available over this period of time. While valuing the tools, I have also despaired as I recognized their limitations. There were several problems. First these tools did not work well even for the pastor. Their effectiveness, was especially limited if you were an outsider, and had not earned the right to be heard. That could take years, especially for the pastor. Second, in many congregations, nearly all the believer's friends were in the church, they had no meaningful contact with unbelievers. Third, while I could effectively preach the word, I did not yet have a clear understanding of what the ministry of my congregation was to be or how to equip them for it.

Finally after pastoring 3 churches over a period of 12 years, I made the decision to get some answers. Rather, than study independently, I choose to go back to school. I did this while pastoring yet another church. I graduated in 1983, having devoted virtually every class to studying the ministry of the laity, (i.e., a course on the book of Act, became a study of lay people in the early Church), regardless of the subject, ending with a master's thesis "The Ministry of the Laity in its Social Contact as it Effects Evangelism"

I might have thought this prepared me to make healthy changes, and have a fruitful pastoral ministry. I do not believe God thought I was adequately prepared. I believe now that God wanted me to spend many years, learning to be an effective layperson. In effect, to really come to a clear understanding of the role God wants His people, the **body of Christ** to play in the world they inhabit.

In 1986, I became self-employed in construction. I fully expected this to be for a year or two at most. While I pastored another 4 years part-time and was very involved in active ministry within the church in the intervening years, often including preaching, I continued to operate my business for 25 years with up to 6 employees.

God taught me much during this time. Sometimes this was just plain fun, at other times it was just plain awful. I struggled with all the issues any one does. I succeeded, I failed. There were many times of dryness when nothing seemed to change. There were times when I knew and experienced God's closeness. There were times when I battled for faith itself. There were times when I despaired at what is called the "Church". There were times when with all its imperfection, the Church was my lifeline.

During this time I attempted to begin writing down what I was learning and to use the material to teach and train others. *The one most important fact I have learned; when you make friends of people that God has already placed around you, love them, listen to them, answer honestly the question they ask, live consistently with them and before them; barriers disappear, including major cultural barriers, and God can use you to see people come to Christ*. I have seen Hindu's and the only Buddhist, with whom I am personally acquainted come to Christ, and I assure you I did not do anything special. Christ could do the same through any committed follower.

While God has many and varied ways of spreading the gospel. Many and varied ways that He works through His people, I have come to strongly believe that His first and primary means is through the **person to person** contacts that virtually everyone has. Even when God wants to broaden an individual's ministry, perhaps even call them to fulltime involvement at some level, **it all starts here in the natural person to person contacts we each have.**

While discussing my involvement in the local church we were then attending; and discussing my approach to evangelism as opposed to what they had practiced; one of the elders observed: one of the primary differences between approaches is that **yours has longevity**. He is correct. We should never love and care for people just to win them to Christ. We should make friends, love and care for people. Period. Genuine love has staying power.

It is my prayer that if it is not already a fact in your life, person to person ministries within your circle of influence will be seen as your first level of ministry regardless of where else He may lead you.

It is my prayer that you will see this ministry as the natural outgrowth of loving God, and loving those that he places around you.

It is my prayer that you will see this ministry not as something that you must do in the same way or with the results that someone else may have, but rather something you can do as no one else can do it, because God himself is in you working through the gifts and person that is uniquely you.

The style of writing changes as I move through the book reflecting the time and circumstances in which it was originally written. A lifetime has been spent with evangelism as a primary focus. In some instances I have summarized basic principles, gleaned from my studies.

With over 50 years of study both of the Word and so many books that, many I cannot remember, at best I can be credited only for assimilating what someone else thought and making it my own. I have tried to give credit for specific information; however there is much in my thinking that I cannot remember its original source.

Have fun and let God teach you, both as you read this book, but also as you check everything in it against the authority of God's word, and adapt them to use as God guides you.

Section One

The Body of Christ:
meant to interact

A Biblical study of the meaning and purpose of the body of Christ

This section is deliberately a serious Study. It is intended to show the biblical and historical foundation on which this book is based. If you are overwhelmed by theology: please read at least the summary at the end of this section and move on to the next section which gives more personal application.

In this book we will almost exclusively refer to the Church as the body of Christ. There are several other terms in scripture by which the church may be described. However almost always when speaking of what the church does, how it is to act, what its function is to be, metaphorically it is described as the body of Christ. The church will be (future) the bride of Christ. Here and now the church invisible is his body on this earth. The body, (our physical body) houses our spirit, it is the dwelling place, the vehicle through which we live in space and time, through which we touch all of nature including each other. Christ's body does the same for him, as he interacts with the world through us when we are allowing him to live fully through us. We who are believers are the body of Christ, we are the physical means by which he interacts as he seeks to save and redeem lost humanity.

"The Church does not have a mission, but God's mission has the Church"
Jo Ann Lyons, Gen. Supt. of The Wesleyan Church; Dakota Dist. Conf. June 24, 2013

The Church (invisible as distinguished from institutionally) is Christ's body, through which he acts through His Spirit to touch people in this world.

1

Old Testament scriptures trace God's plan to redeem man. It starts at the very beginning, from the time of man's fall into sin and separation, through man's own unbelief and rebellion. It traces a line of faith; God's choice of Abram because of his faith, on through to the establishment of Abraham's offspring as a nation, intended to be God's servant to reach the nations.

We pick up an important portion of the story with the nation Israel, and Isaiah's prophecy.

The Body as a Servant

The Jewish nation misunderstood the nature of the promised Messiah. Even the disciples of Jesus failed to fully comprehend. It took the risen Christ Himself to bring the disciples to an understanding of these things.

> He said to them: 'How foolish you are and how slow of heart to believe all that the prophets have spoken! Did not the Christ have to suffer these things then enter his glory?' And beginning with Moses and all the prophets, he explained to them what was said in all the scriptures concerning himself (Luke 24:25-27).

This new understanding was in total contrast to the expectations of the people.

Contrary to their expectation, *the Messiah was to be a suffering servant.* If the Church is to properly understand its role as the body of Christ, it must first understand Christ the servant.

Israel the Servant

We turn to the book of Isaiah for our background for the concept of the servant:

Here is my servant, whom I uphold,

My chosen one in whom I delight;

I will put my Spirit on him

And he will bring justice to the nations.

He will not shout or cry out,

Or raise his voice in the streets.

A bruised reed he will not break,

And a smoldering wick he will not snuff out.

In faithfulness he will bring forth justice;

He will not falter or be discouraged till he

establishes justice on the earth.

In his law the islands will put their hope

(Isa. 43:1-4)

Tentatively the servant is identified as Israel in the following verse; "But now listen, O Jacob, my servant, whom I have chosen" (Isa. 44:1). But Israel as a servant nation is found a failure;

Here, you deaf; look, you blind, and

see!   Who is blind but my servant,

and deaf like the messenger I send?

Who is blind like the one committed to me,

Blind like the servant of the Lord?

You have seen many things,

but have not paid attention;

> Your ears are open, but you hear nothing

> (Isa. 43:18-20)

Later we see the servant again identified. But this time the servant appears to be only a remnant of Israel.

He said to me, 'you are my servant,

> Israel, in whom I will display my splendor.'

But I said, 'I have labored to no purpose;

> I have spent my strength in vain and for nothing.' He says:

'It is too small a thing for you to be my servant

> To restore the tribes of Jacob

> And bring back those of Israel I have kept.

I will also make you a light for the Gentiles,

> That you may bring my salvation to the ends of the earth'

(Isa. 49:3-4, 6).

The picture which emerges at this point is that God has called the nation of Israel to be his servant to bring the message of salvation to the nations of the world. God has asked the nation of Israel to obey (Isa. 44:1; cf. 65:12). He has asked for them to endure (Isa. 43:1-6). He has asked them to witness (43:12). Israel as a whole refused to obey, they wanted anything but the suffering that endurance required, and instead of witnessing to the glory of God, they gave way instead to serving idols. So the task is then given to the faithful few who remained true within Israel, yet who still do not accept the implications of the task God has given them.

Discussion questions;

How is the church today like Israel of the OT?

How am I, how is my local church like Israel?

What character did God seek, what did He receive?

What place does sacrifice and suffering play?

How does this fit with blessing and reward?

Christ the Servant

The difficulty with interpreting who the servant is in this portion of Isaiah is that the servant is increasingly portrayed in a personal way. While in some places the servant is identified with Israel (Isa.41:8; 44:1-2; 45:4; 48:20; 49:3). In other places the servant is a personification, especially in 52:13 through 53:12, the servant is so individualized that commentators generally agree that this is a prophecy that could only be fulfilled by Jesus Christ.

As we look at the whole of Isaiah Chapters 41-53 we see that the servant of the Lord represents both the Lord and His people. These are so closely related that they may be seen as the head and a body. Thus we look forward even here to the Church as the body of Christ, with Christ Himself as its head.

We error greatly if we think that by simply identifying the servant, we have come to understand the significance of this section of Scripture. The primary meaning is to be discovered in the nature and purpose of servanthood. We are to remember that "he will bring justice to the nations;" he is to be "a light for the Gentiles;" he is "to open the eyes that are blind, free captives from prison and release from the dungeon those who sit in darkness."

The nature of servanthood comes into sharpest focus when we consider Isaiah 53. There we see the servant gives up his own life in order to take up our infirmities, and carry our sorrows; we see Him pierced for our transgressions, and crushed for our iniquities. The Lord laid on him the iniquity of us all and by his wounds we are healed.

The ministry of Jesus is continually marked by the Old Testament themes of *utter obedience, fearless witness, and innocent suffering,* all of which are a fulfilment of the conception of the Servant pictured in the Old Testament. The concepts of the servant are never far from Jesus mind; they become the clear focus toward the end. ***He consummates the role of the servant in word and deed as he goes to the cross.***

These scriptures do not make reference to the concept of Love, however, we cannot understand Jesus's command to love except in the context of His own love for the world.

The Church as the Servant

Did God intend that **servanthood** should end with His Son Jesus Christ? We answer that question with another. Has the mission for which Jesus Christ came into the world been accomplished? We find our answer to this question in these words of Jesus Christ: "As you sent me into the world, I have sent them into the world" (John 17:18).

At this point we should perhaps understand the Church as the **community** of those sent into the world to complete the mission of Jesus Christ. We might compare the servanthood pictured by Isaiah to an hourglass. It began with the corporate people of God or Israel. It narrowed to the person of Jesus Christ. It expanded again to include the corporate body of Christ, the Church.

Sheri was a young woman from a foreign country. While her husband worked on doctorate at the local university she was completing a third Masters at another university. We had become friends over time. One of the needs we had discovered was transportation. Since they had no car getting groceries was particularly difficult, particularly in the ice and snow. For many months my wife Sue weekly took her along grocery shopping, going several miles out of the way each time. This simple act of service was just one of the facts that cemented our friendship, a friendship that eventually led to Sheri seeking Christ.

As we examine the New Testament Scriptures, especially the words of Christ himself, it is abundantly clear that he intended for His disciples to follow Him in the matter of servanthood. "If anyone wants to be first, he must be the very last, and the servant of all" (Mark 9:35). In contrast to the way of the Gentiles, Jesus instructs His disciples: "the greatest among you should be like the youngest and the one who rules like the one who serves" (Luke 22:26).

In employing the word translated service in these verses, Jesus chose one that is uncharacteristic of Old Testament Scripture, and one that was not used in this sense in the Jewish or Hellenistic environment. He clearly avoids the use of words which express a relationship of rulers and ruled. Jesus clearly was not concerned with mere table service or care for bodily needs, rather the origins of the word <u>diakonia,</u> shows that <u>a completely personal service was intended</u>. God wants to be with his people, working in and through them. We also are to be with people. We are not to merely do actions of service, but to be <u>personally involved</u> with people.

A pastor of my acquaintance visited an uncommitted parishioner, the parishioner was in the midst of placing rings in the noses of several young pigs. The pastor asked for some old clothes to put on and got in and assisted with the job. A later pastor of the same church, finding this same parishioner similarly busy, demanded that he quit and set down for a visit. Who demonstrated a servant likeness to Christ? Which was most likely to be heard when he spoke?

Michael Green in <u>Called to Serve</u> says "Christian life begins when we allow Jesus to be our servant. It continues as, incorporated into Christ, we share the role of Servant which He made so much His own." Green, Michael, <u>Called to serve, Ministry and Ministers in the Church. Christian Foundations, Vol.1</u> Philadelphia; The Westminster Press, 1964

The Jewish view of servant in Isaiah as the corporate body of Israel, may well be the germ of the idea which led to the use of the metaphor of the body in the New Testament. Since clearly the Body –idea exist in the Old Testament, it is not at all surprising that following the resurrection, once the eye of faith has taken hold of who Jesus really is, once they began to take hold of his instructions to them, they would also see themselves as collectively his body here on this earth.

Some of the most basic meaning and purpose of the Church as the body of Christ is contained in the concept of Servanthood. This servanthood becomes fully expressed as Christ the servant takes on flesh <u>in the world</u> through the Church as servant.

Use of the words, <u>in the world</u> is deliberate. The Church too often understands servanthood as, in the Church, to the Church, rather than by the Church, <u>in the world.</u>

This is vividly seen in the fact that even in "successful churches" the training and discipling of its peoples is almost exclusively oriented around what they will do in the church. <u>Rarely is the central focus on equipping them for their ministry in the office, the factory, or the market place.</u>

One of the issues faced by pastors attempting to equip is the reality that most of them have never lived in the office, factory, or market place. Consequently they lack the confidence to approach this area. Yet a pastor in humble relationship with growing disciples can in working together with these disciples, find ways these problems can be overcome. This will require time and effort, but if equipping people for their ministry is a priority, with God's help it can be done.

In Christ's teachings, parables, stories we find a wealth of information that will instruct our attitudes and character and thus equip believers for a life of service that the Spirit can use as he lives through us.

The church can never duplicate the servanthood of Jesus Christ as it relates to His sacrificial death for the sins of mankind. Nor does it need to. The atonement was finished on the Cross of Christ. However, the Church is continually called upon to take up its cross, to deny itself, to be a servant.

This call, is to become living sacrifices, even as the apostle Paul describes in Romans 12:1-2. Christians are called upon to die to self in order that Christ may live fully in and through them.

Discussion questions:

What does it really mean to be a servant, how does this apply in our generation? Individually? Corporately?

What does servanthood have to do with Evangelism? What does it have to do with speaking the words of the gospel?

How have you been equipped? How do you wish you were equipped?

How have you equipped others for their ministry in the world in which they live every day?

What resources, collaboration with others, interaction within the body would make this equipping possible?

What would Servanthood look like in the local Church?

What would Servanthood look like among the believers; believers immersed in the world?

How am I succeeding, How am I failing to fulfill the role Christ wants for me personally?

The Body of Christ and Unity

The concept of the Church as the body of Christ in relation to servanthood is neglected and little understood. However as a metaphor to describe unity in the Church, the concept, the body has been widespread. In the 60's the concept of body of Christ was universal, and so dominated Christian thinking that a number of church mergers took place. The Ecumenical Movement of that day rightfully drew attention to the metaphor "the body" in support of the unity of the Church.

The unity of the Church rightfully should be held high in our list of important doctrines. Christ himself in one of his final recorded prayers, prayed: "May they be brought to complete unity to let the world know that you sent me and have loved them even as you have loved me" (John 17:23). Jesus coupled the unity of His body the Church with the world's recognition of who He was as the Son sent from God, thus coupling it with His whole purpose in coming to this world. We should do no less.

Nevertheless we must question the motives for which unity is sought. Was unity sought as a means to an end, or is unity an end in itself?

God's purpose in Unity

In each of the books, Romans, Corinthians, Ephesians, and Colossians, the metaphor of the body is introduced at least in part to deal with the twin problems of strife and individualistic patterns of behavior. But why was it important to deal with these problems? The importance lies in the fact that **these problems prohibit the Church from effectively accomplishing its mission.** As Jesus prayed for his disciples, He spoke thus to his Father: "As you have sent me into the world, I have sent them into the world" (John 17:18). Again as noted earlier He continues, "May they be brought to complete unity to let the world know that you sent me and that I have loved them even as you have loved me" (John 17:23).

The purpose of the unity of the Church is mission. That mission can be totally jeopardized by lack of unity. "Every kingdom divided against itself will be ruined, and every city or household divided against itself will not stand" (Matt. 12:25).

Yet in U. S. churches there is such lack of unity, often such separation from each other, such isolation from one another, such vying to be the only denomination that is correct; that <u>often unbelievers, ignorant in the ways</u> <u>of the church, equate each one as</u> <u>another religion.</u> There is little if any distinction between individual Christian denominations and other world religions such as Hindu, Muslim, and Buddhist.

If the purpose of the unity of the Church is mission, what is the nature of its mission?

(1) It is God purpose to redeem man and restore man to the place for which He originally created him. A place wherein man can again have fellowship with God. Man is to again bear the divine image (Rom. 8:28; I John 3:2). This is more than simply Justification, (I get God, and get right with God), it is also:

(2) Sanctification (overcoming our character flaws through the grace and power of God, because God gets me). It involves the total of all that is part of God's plan in our lives.

(3) "The creation itself will be liberated from its bondage to decay and brought into the glorious freedom of the children of God (Rom. 8:21). This is not an after-thought with God. Sin has brought terrible disruption to the total of this world. God plans to restore the harmony he planned.

The unity of the Church (the body of Christ) is essential if this gospel (incredibly good news) is to be credible to the world.

It is important to be completely clear as to the mission at this point. Jesus Christ through His own death and resurrection has already completed all that is necessary for our salvation, *but it remains for His body the Church* *to make Him known.*

It remains for the Church, united in faith and life to be ministers of reconciliation, that the world may be reconciled to God. Jesus prayed that they may be one, that they may be brought to complete unity. He prayed thus, that the world may believe.

The mission to be accomplished through the united witness of those who make up his body, both through its work and word, is that the world may

11

come to believe in Jesus Christ and thus may participate in the abundant life which he offers.

The restoration of **humanity** to the divine image is at the center and of greatest importance; however it is not the whole of God's plan. It is only the starting point from which God plans to move toward the accomplishment of His whole redemptive plan.

The second part of God mission shows God full purpose: the restoration of the **universe** to the divine plan. Jesus taught us to pray, "your kingdom come, your will be done on earth as it is in heaven (Matt. 6:10). This prayer immediately confirms Jesus broader understanding of God's plan than most of us give credit.

The kingdom is both here and now, as well as culminating later with Christ's return. As already stated: A full-orbed plan of redemption is not afterthought with God. Paul writing to the Church at Ephesus describes in broad outline, yet with much detail, Gods plan for the ages.

> He chose us in Him before the creation of the world . . . He made known to us the mystery of His will . . . which He purposed in Christ, to be put into effect when the times will have reached their fulfillment__ to bring all things in heaven and earth together under one head, even Christ (Eph. 1:4, 9-10).

The 'cosmic perspective' becomes particularly clear when Paul begins to speak of God's power:

> "which he exerted in Christ when he raised him from the dead and seated him at his right hand in the heavenly realms, far above all rule and authority and power and dominion, and every title that can be given, not only in the present age but also in the one to come. And God placed all things under his feet and appointed him to be head over everything for the Church which is His body, the fullness of him who fills everything in every way (Eph. 1:20-23)

From this perspective the unity of the Church can never be an end in itself. Scripturally the unity of the Church is always unity with a purpose. That purpose is crystal clear, the mission of redeeming mankind and the universe in which we live. It is God's purpose to unite in Christ, men and women of every race and culture "to do good works which God prepared in advance for us to do" (Eph. 2:10).

The basis of unity in the body of Christ

"The body is a unit, though it is made up of many parts and though all its parts are many, they form one body. So it is with Christ" (I Cor. 12:12). The question is what is the basis of this unity?

The answer is to be found in the unity and purpose of God Himself. Note, for example: "There are different kinds of working, but the same God works all of them in all men" (I Cor. 12:4-6)

We see here an example of the unity of the Godhead. We see also the pulling together of gifts, service and working of all men. The clear implication is that there is one God who harmonizes the efforts of all men to accomplish a single purpose.

There is more here however, than singleness of purpose. There is a common source of life, Jesus Christ Himself. Even as the branches in a vine have life because of the vine to which they are attached.

"For we were all baptized by the one Spirit into one body – whether Jews or Greeks, slave or free – and we were all given the one Spirit to drink" (I Cor. 12:13). Thus we have here not only unit of purpose, but unity of life itself. We are all one because we are "in Christ" "Therefore, if anyone is in Christ, he is a new creation" (II Cor. 5:17). **The experience of being in Christ is central to an understanding of the meaning of the metaphor of the Body of Christ.**

The Experience of being "in Christ" is one of **two parallel relationships** that form the basis of unity in the body of Christ. (1) **In Christ we have**

shared life with other believers. Believers are not only united to Christ, but through Him to each other.

We become a collective society of those who are "in Christ". Because of whom Christ is: his love, his power, his forgiveness, His cleansing; the experience of being in Him tends to break down all barriers, and abolish all separateness.

However, we all know what it is like to be part of a family. Families do quarrel.

In his first letter to the Corinthians, Paul asks: "Is Christ divided? Was Paul crucified for you? Were you baptized into the name of Paul?" (I Cor. 1:13).

If Christ is one, as Paul implies, and we individually and corporately are in Christ, then we have a basis for unity. So then why don't we always have unity? Why is the Church, so often divided?

Perhaps the answer lies with the second parallel relationship we have in the body of Christ. (2) This second relationship has to do with authority in the Body of Christ. **This second relationship has to do with Christ as the head of His body.**

The mystery of God's grace to us is great. God obviously extends grace to his children, even when they remain childish beyond childhood. It was so at Corinth. There were those at Corinth who though they were "in Christ . . . [were] mere infants in Christ . . .," were not taking their instructions from Christ.

We do not take it lightly if portions of our body do not respond to instructions from the head. When they don't, it is at best annoying, at worst it may be life threatening.

Whenever as at Corinth, believers are still behaving like "mere men" rather than accepting the headship of Christ; there will also still remain quarreling and divisions among us. All the attendant damage strife causes to the mission of Christ, will continue to the extent that we fail to allow Christ to be head.

It is a serious question, as to how long one may remain a member of the body of Christ, and fail to accept orders from the head of the body. It raises even greater questions when local units of the Church refuse to accept the authority of Christ. The church which refuses the authority of Christ and becomes its own authority ultimately ceases to be the Church. The body can only exist through its life in Him.

Our primary concern, however at this point is the basis of unity in the body of Christ. It is safe to say, **the body will be fully united when the body is fully surrendered to Christ as its head.** It will be united or disunited in direct proportion to its acceptance of Christ as its head.

By this, the writer does not mean to say, there will be no significant doctrinal or practical disagreements. Rather, we are speaking of a unity of purpose around the central and pivotal truths of the faith in Christ. We are speaking of unity around pivotal truths that are so clearly stated in the scriptures that in any *Bible* believing group of believers across the globe or any section of church, you will still find them taught. We are also speaking about unity because of the common of life and fellowship we find with those "in Christ" regardless of denominational distinctives, as we live together in the love of Christ.

Groups, i.e., local Churches in a community, denominations, etc. which want to work together in harmony and effectiveness in reaching their communities will keep these central truths visible in their public emphasis. At the same time they will downplay, keep in the background those doctrines, which are not central and pivotal to the Christian faith.

Discussion Questions:

State as clearly as possible Christ reason for wanting unity in the Church, that is his body here on this earth.

Does the Church as you know it from personal experience understand God's purpose in the unity of the Church?

If our unity comes from our commonness of life, because of being "in Christ" with the common head of Christ Himself, why is there disunity and what will bring unity?

What difficulty does the average Christian face when confronting Christ as the head of the Church, as their own head? Is this more difficult in a freedom oriented society?

Is it really possible to disagree about many issues while having unity around core issues and the overall purpose of the gospel?

Can God's power enable us to love one another in spite of our disagreements and thus make Christ attractive to the world?

The Body as the Infleshment of Christ in the World

"Infleshment" a term meant to describe the means by which Christ clothes Himself in human flesh in the world today.

> **The church is Christ's body meant to interact in this world as the visible presence of Christ himself; the means by which He is literally present in this world through the Holy Spirit to continue the process of reconciling individuals to Himself.**

When we look at the biblical concept of being "in Christ" we are looking at only one side of the coin. The Scriptures speak clearly not only of the relationship of being in Christ, but also of **Christ being in the believer.** One of the clearest expressions of this concept is found in Paul's words to the Galatians. "I have been crucified with Christ and **I no long live, but Christ lives in me.** The life I live in the body, I live by faith in the Son of God, who loves me and gave Himself for me".
(Gal. 2:20)

The phrases "in Christ" and "Christ in you", describe the mystical union between Christ and His Church. This union is at the heart of the Church's relationship to Christ and His body.

But how far can a person take the metaphor of the body without having an illegitimate extension of the metaphor? Bible scholars are divided on this issue. Some see in the Church a continuation of the incarnation. Others react strongly against such a suggestion. The division centers on the understanding of the meaning of the phrase "extension of the incarnation", and the understanding of the authority of the Church. This writer does not intend to solve the controversy, rather to put within definite limits his understanding and use of this concept.

What are the limiting factors in understanding the concept of the Church as an "extension of the incarnation"? First this writer prefers the phrase, the infleshment of Christ in the world. Second, the phrase is used only of the means with which Christ continues to have contact with world through His Spirit as He indwells believers throughout the world. To confuse this with questions related to the atonement, etc. would be to miss the point entirely. Neither should there be any thought that Christ is bodily present. Christ rose from the dead, and bodily ascended to heaven. He is not present in his earthly body.

Third, **our understanding is within the definite limitations of the Church as Christ's body, in relation to Christ's headship.** If the church refuses to obey its head, then Christ is not touching the world through it, or at least very imperfectly. Christ not only is head of the Church, He is its very source of life. While there is an inter-relationship between Christ and His Church, the two are by no means identical. Fourth, the Church must continually return to the Scriptures as our final authority, both for our understanding of the Church and also for our understanding of Christ Himself

What then is the significance of the body of Christ as an infleshment, or visible touching presence of Christ in the world?

Often the Church is viewed more simply as the people of God. In this view the church is more a people chosen by God who are journeying through, who are attempting to make it safely to heavens shore where they will be safe evermore.

However it is through the Church as the body of Christ that we recognize the kingdom of God as not only future, but also here and present now. Jesus said; "The kingdom of God is within you" (Luke 17:21). As the bride of Christ the Church will be part of the eschatological kingdom. The key here is "will be". The Church will be the bride of Christ.

As the body of Christ, not only is the Church presently part of the kingdom of God which has already broken into the kingdoms of this world, but **through His body, the Church, Christ is present in this world to finish His work.**

In this present evil age the Church is to display the life and fellowship of the age to come. The Church lives as dual citizens, it still lives in this age, made up of people who are sinful mortal men. The Church is made of citizens who in this age will never reach perfection, yet it also displays in foretaste, the life of the perfect order of Gods Kingdom, which is here, yet is to come. Here we see clearly not only the individual witness to Christ's life giving and transforming power, we also see the beauty of the whole.

Discussion Questions:

In contrast to the world around us, what should a person who lives "in Christ" and Christ is living in them, look like?

Describe their character traits. What stories of Jesus illustrate these traits?

How is doing life Jesus way different than presumptuous grace, legalism, or trying to earn salvation?

The primacy of the Body Metaphor

We are investigating the manner in which Christ is present in the world today. Our conclusion is that essentially **Christ in his personhood; is**

only present in the world today, as he is infleshed by, or takes on flesh, through those who allow Him to fully live in and through them, as His Spirit indwells their hearts. God's methods in the world have consistently been through people. "In the past God spoke to our forefathers through the prophets at many times and in various ways, but in these last days he has spoken to us by his son" (Heb. 1:1-2). At the present, it is God's purpose to reveal Himself through his body, the Church.

<u>The Church in the here and now is always and only specifically spoken of as the body of Christ.</u> There are countless references which speak of people and their relationship to God and his kingdom. They are referred to as the people of God, the temple of God, a royal priesthood. Yet while it is proper that these pictures should influence our thinking concerning the Church, they are never given in scriptures as a description of the Church itself.

This fact lends force to the need to keep clear the biblical understanding of the Church as the body of Christ. We acknowledge that it is a metaphor, but God is not accidental in his choice of words. As already noted, arguments for understanding the body of Christ as an infleshment of Christ in this world are drawn from and strengthened by many other facts found in the Word of God; first, is the continual emphasis on servanthood. Second, we see that the concept of infleshment is originated by Christ Himself, prior to Paul's conception of the Church as the body of Christ.

We see this conception in Christ's description of the vine and the branches in John 15. We see it again as Christ describes in John 17 His relationship with the Father, and with the disciples. We see it once more in the promise of the coming of the Holy Spirit who not only shall be with you, but will be in you.

It is God's purpose to be in the world through the Church. The Church does not exist for itself. In fact the Church does not exist for God alone. **The Church exists as God's chosen instrument to bring the world back to Himself.**

As the body of Christ, it exists to make Him known.

However profound a sermon,

However solemn and act of worship,

However well - organized a system of pastoral care,

However methodical an instruction,

However ingenious a theology,

However effective a charity –

There is no value in all of this if it is done in

The isolation of a self-congratulating community,

Of a church which lives only for itself.

Kung, Hans, <u>The Church,</u> Garden City, NY: Image Books, 1975, P 619-620

Gifts within the Body of Christ:
The Purpose behind Gifts

Summarizing our conclusions to this point, we note, all of God's people are called to ministry. <u>Some of these are especially set apart to equip or enable the others for their ministry.</u> The primary biblical description of the Church is that it is the body of Christ. As such it is God's means by which Christ is to be clothed in human flesh to act in this present world. This being true, the questions must be answered. Why would he do this? **What is His purpose in infleshing Himself in the believer, and how then does God intend to accomplish this infleshment?** Rephrasing this. What is his purpose in living in and through the believer, and how then does God intend to accomplish this?

Picture for yourself, the overwhelming task that Jesus is giving to the disciples; picture their insignificance as men even in their generation. "They took note that they were unschooled, ordinary men," Acts 4:13

When we really see the size and scope of the global mandate that Jesus was leaving with his disciples, we will quickly see the absolute necessity of something more than our scanty human resources.

When we take a close look at the typical Church today we also see the absolute need. In many instances we may be having good fellowship, have an active program, we may even be conserving our biological growth, **but we are barely scratching the surface in reaching, unsaved adults and their families**. In the average U. S. church we are going backward.

Growing local churches often give the impression that they are reaching many new people, because we see new families in church. Yet even there we need to check and see how many of these families are just new to our local church. We may be growing in numbers as a congregation, but **are we seeing new converts**.

At one point I worshiped for a period of 5 years with a congregation of godly people. We became very effective in attracting large numbers of Christ followers moving into the community or seeking a new church home. Not until the final year did we see any one new choose to trust Christ. Yet because of the large numbers of new families, there was great satisfaction and contented feeling that all was great.

In direct contrast to this typical lack, observe history immediately following Pentecost. The actions of the church following Pentecost stand out in bold relief.

Yet the story in the book of Acts is still His story. Jesus had specifically told them, that he would not leave them "as orphans; I will come to you" (John 14:18). **The power, the influence, the magnetism, the vitality, found**

in Jesus is to continue in His disciples as Jesus Himself indwells them through His Spirit.

Acts is an account of accomplishments made in the power and force of the Holy Spirit (His Spirit). Yet it is still Jesus story. So great were the effects of the witness of the early Church as empowered by the Holy Spirit, that the enemies at Thessalonica charged, "These that have turned the world upside down are come hither also"(Acts 17:6b).

The life of Jesus goes on in and through His Church. Christ is still alive, He still acts. In fact, Jesus says; "anyone who has faith in me will do what I have been doing. He will do even greater things than these, because I am going to the Father. And I will do whatever you ask in my name, so that the Son may bring glory to the Father (John 14:12-13).

Support for the position that Jesus life goes on in and through the Church is seen clearly in both the Book of Acts, and also in John's gospel where we find some of the most intimate conversations with his disciples as he prepares them immediately preceding His death. As we meditate carefully on John 13-17, we see **answers emerge to the why, what, and how questions**.

In these Chapters we discover the following;

(1) Jesus is planning to leave this earth and return to the Father (John 14:2, 12, 28; 16:15, 28; 17:11).

(2) The Holy Spirit will come to be <u>with</u> the disciples (John 14:16, 26; 16:7).

(3) Jesus plans to be <u>in</u> the disciples after he is gone (John 14:18-20, 23; 15:5-7; 15:15; 17:23, 26).

(4) The Holy Spirit will not only be <u>with</u> the disciples but also <u>in</u> them (John 14:16-17, 26; 15:26; 16:7, 13).

(5) The Holy Spirit will bear witness to Jesus (teach and remind) in the lives of the disciples (John 14:26; 15:26; 16:13-15).

(6) The disciples are to bear witness to Jesus in the world (John 14:12; John Chapter 15 especially verses 14-16 and 27; John 17:18).

(7) The disciples are to receive adequate resources to do the work He gives them (John 14:13-14; 15:7, 16; 16:23-24).

(8) The only purpose for being in the vine is to bear fruit. Reproduce. (John 15:2, 5, 8, 16)

(9) The disciples are absolutely powerless and cannot bear fruit if they are not abiding in Christ (John 15:4-6).

(10) The Holy Spirit will convince the world of its guilt (John 16:8-11)

We cannot properly understand these statements or this section of Scripture unless we also come to an understanding and acceptance of God as a triune God; One God in three persons, Father, Son, and Holy Spirit.

We also cannot properly comprehend these Scriptures without an understanding of Christ's infleshment in the world today through His disciples. Try if you will to view the task of spreading the good news of Christ's redemptive power to the entire world. How would you do it? These passages make one thing clear. **Jesus intended to do it by himself being present in His disciples through the Holy Spirit, and through them to complete the mission of reconciliation of the world to Himself.**

Christ as a man was one person at one point in time. At best, without the use of modern media, or transportation, he was able to be in contact with a few thousand people at any one time and place. He could only be close friends with a handful of people. In these respects he was limited as a man, even as we are.

For example, as a man Billy Graham has had an impact on a larger group of people than Jesus Christ. Yet Billy Graham was still just one man with a limited impact.

Now, however, Jesus Christ intends leave this earth, but he is going to expand His ministry by indwelling every person who puts their trust in Him. Through His body the Church, Christ is going to continue His ministry. He will no longer, be limited to one time and place. Instead, through His body the Church, He will begin to permeate the world at every level of society. He will be everywhere people are, redeeming people, one person at a time, filling them with his love and power and sending them forth to touch yet one more person with is love and grace.

Consider the following:

Work for 31 days. Choose your wages: $50,000. Per day, or start with $.01 and double your wages every day. $50,000 X 31 = $1,550,000 or by doubling your wages every day you will receive $2,147,483,648.00, or $1,073,741,824 on the last day alone. The difference is between addition and multiplication. <u>Jesus chose to invest Himself primarily in a few and to multiply Himself through those truly committed to Him.</u>

Consider the implications in our world today:

World population: Approximately 7.2 Billion.

Currently there are approximately 2.1 Billion Christians; 1.6 Billion Islam; 1.1 Billion Secular (I.E. No organized religion); 1 Billion Hinduism; 1.4 Billion, other religions.

How are they to be reached?

Assume that only 700,000 of the world's 2.1 Billion Christians are active in their faith: that indicates a ratio of 1 to 10 people. In other words there is one active Christian in the world for every 10 people in the world.

Can you relate with unconditional love to 10 people in such a way as to communicate the essence of the gospel in your lifetime?

Will you allow yourself to become a fully devoted and discipled follower of Jesus Christ such that this can happen?

Who has God placed around you, or who does He want to place around you right now?

Jesus did not send his disciples out to do the impossible task of making disciples of all nations. He sent them out to live in Him, so He could live in them and through them make disciples of all nations.

The Gift, the Holy Spirit Himself

We turn our full attention then to the Holy Spirit for it is He who is the gift which Jesus promised. <u>He Himself is more important than any gifts which He may</u> <u>bestow.</u>

Who is He?

He is the third person of the triune God. He is the active person who administers that which God purposes. He is the counselor, the comforter, the one who represents the ascended Christ to us. He glorifies Christ by perpetuating His character, bringing about Christ's kingdom, and fulfilling his ongoing redeeming purpose in the world.

There are many symbols in the Scripture that help us to see more clearly who this unique person is; he is symbolized as breath, or wind, even as the Spirit breathed into man the breath of life. He is symbolized as water, as in the waters of life; as fire, particularly in the area of purifying or cleansing. He is seen as oil, as a dove, and as a seal, suggesting among other things his role in preserving.

The Spirit of God is seen actively in the whole of Jesus life and ministry, in the bringing of redemption to man. This is clearly described all the way from His birth, his temptation, it is clearly seen in Jesus reliance on Him throughout his life. **This is particularly important as we realize that Jesus was promising to us his disciples, this same Spirit that had sustained and empowered Him.** God become flesh at one point in historical time; but he through this same Spirit, takes on flesh as he indwells and empowers every believer as they begin to be conformed to the image of Christ by this same Spirit, and allow Christ to live in and through them.

There are **three primary means** by which God intends to work through the Holy Spirit in the body of Christ.

The **presence** of Christ in the life of the believer, <u>through the Holy Spirit</u>

God in and through his Son Jesus Christ intends to be fully present in the life of the believer through the Holy Spirit. This presence was to have an impact that even His physical presence could not.

> Speaking of the difference between the <u>physical presence of Christ</u> with the disciples, and <u>His presence with the disciples through the Holy Spirit</u> whom Christ promised, Dr. Charles W. Carter well states:

> "The Spirit's presence was to be to the believer what it was not possible for His earthly presence to be. In His earthly presence Christ could meet with His disciples, have fellowship with them, and teach them. However of necessity His relation to them was inconstant at any given time . . . . the Spirit, unlimited by bodily form, could be omnipresent. He could, by His very nature as Spirit be the constant companion of the believer's lives. His presence would be the internal experience of the disciples by reason of His indwelling of their spiritual natures. And His presence would be an abiding experience as He was to be God's permanent gift to all believers." Carter, Charles W. <u>Person and Ministry of the Holy Spirit, A Wesleyan Perspective</u>. Grand Rapids, MI: Baker Book House, 1974

However Christ intends to be present for more than just the believer's personal assistance.

While having Christ present through the Holy Spirit is and should be comforting to the believer, it is not an end in itself. **Christ intends, by living in the believer, to also be present in this world**, such that when we are in contact with those around us, he also is in contact through us.

> **As Christ Himself is present in us, He is present and touching those we touch.**

Purity in the heart of the believer through the Holy Spirit

The Holy Spirit also brings purity to the heart of the believer. This is purity where we are in fact pure because of our surrender to and continual cleansing by His Spirit. There will thus be the refreshing sweet smelling aroma to those in contact with these believers. Purity represents what we are when we are fully surrendered unto the Lord, thus avoiding a contradiction in presenting Christ to the world. Purity is most clearly demonstrated through our love for others; without love we present a contradiction to the world, for God is love.

We should not assume that this purity is a once and forever one time experience. Rather that it is one in which the vessel itself is in the process of being transformed, and is being used in the midst of a sinful world, and thus requires continuous cleansing.

We must "walk in the light as he is in the light" and thus be purified from all sin. (See 1 John 1) Keep in mind that this is not simply an action of the Holy Spirit independent of our participation. We are transformed by the renewing of our minds. Rom. 12: 1-2. We must be willing, direct and active participants. Thus constantly seeking truth through His word is essential.

Heart purity has more to do with continual cleansing by staying in a living relationship of love with God in which His Spirit is continually present, than any past experience. It has absolutely nothing to do with simply muscling up to be "good"! See the later discussion in "Our Interaction with Christ."

The apostle Peter reveals truth related to heart purity in the following incident: "God, who knows the heart, showed that he accepted them by giving the Holy Spirit to them, just as he did to us. He made no distinction between us and them, for he purified their hearts by faith" (Acts 15:8-9).

The importance of heart purity is made clear by the number and variety of commands: "offer . . . leading to holiness" (Rom.6:19); "be holy" (I Peter 1:15); "goal of this command is love, which comes from a pure heart" (I Timothy 1:5); "be perfect" (Matt. 5:48). Its importance is also underlined by the fact that it is essential for entrance into heaven; "without holiness no one will see the Lord" (Heb. 12:14).

If the reason for heart purity were personal only, no one else would be affected if a person neglected until late in life to be concerned about it. However heart purity relates not only to a man's acceptability to God, but is intimately related to each person's witness of Christ to the world. This positive effect starts with our families and works outward, as the power of sin is broken.

As stated earlier, purity is most clearly demonstrated through our love for others; without purity of heart, the Christian presents a contradiction to the world, for God is love. Purity represents what we are when we are fully surrendered unto the Lord, thus avoiding a contradiction in presenting Christ to the world.

In light of the effect that purity has on the mission of Christ, the admonitions of Scripture take on added importance. Ephesians 4:11-16, gives insight into the nature and purpose of the Church. His admonition immediately following is instructive.

> So I tell you this and insist on it in the Lord, that you must no longer live as "the Gentiles do, in the futility of their thinking - - - put off your old self - - - put on your new self, created to be like God in true righteousness and holiness (Eph. 4:17, 22-23). Be imitators of God, therefore, as dearly loved children and live a life of love, just as Christ loved us and gave himself up for us as a fragrant offering and sacrifice to God (Eph. 5:1-2).

We are not made pure simply to remove some of the consequences of past sin and thus be allowed to pursue our will without hindrance. This would be both a misuse of the power of God and a misunderstanding of purity. It is a mis-understanding of purity because it fails to recognize that **the enthronement of self in the life is the essence of impurity** from which we need to be cleansed. It is a misuse of the power of God, because God's purpose is to use each person made pure as a witness to salvation through Jesus Christ.

God through His Spirit makes the heart pure when a person comes to Him in faith and willingly surrenders themselves fully unto Him. This surrender and resulting power is an absolute essential to fruitfulness and effectiveness in the kingdom of God. <u>God will not give His power to one who cannot be trusted to obey Him.</u> The "holy Spirit is given to those who obey Him" (Acts 5:32). For the Holy Spirit to withhold himself from working through us is to leave us totally incapable of anything except works of the flesh. We may build great buildings, do good deeds, and have large crowds, But we can do nothing of a spiritual nature, have lasting fruit, apart from the Spirit of God; "Apart from me you can do nothing" (John15:5).

Surrender may not lead to dramatic results, but it will always lead to God being able to effectively use us in the way that he wants and sees is best. Whether God chooses to use us in a lowly manner, or in a flashy manner, we are equally of value to him, and equally essential to his purpose.

Power in the life of the believer <u>through the Holy Spirit</u>

Not only is the task of making disciples of all nation not a task that was given to a few specialist, it was and is a task that cannot be done in human strength.

The importance of the **power of the Holy Spirit in the life of the believer**, is underscored by Jesus specific command to his disciples: "do not leave Jerusalem, but wait for the gift my Father promised, which you heard me speak about" (Acts 1:4) He then explains "John baptized with water, but in a few days you will be baptized with the Holy Spirit" (Acts 1:5). He further explains, "you will receive power when the Holy Spirit comes one you; and you will be my witnesses in Jerusalem and in all Judea, and Samaria, and to the ends of the earth" (Acts 1:8)

We should **see the progression here.** The disciples were obedient to the command of Christ to wait in Jerusalem for the gift the Father had promised. This implies both faith in God for their future, and submission to God. Following their obedience, the Holy Spirit was given. The implication for us today is clear. If we desire the Holy Spirit in our lives, we need to begin walking in obedience to the <u>light God has already given.</u>

Through the Holy Spirit, there is power in the life of the believer, life giving power, even as there is power in the seed that is sown, which dies and produces after itself.

Power of the Holy Spirit is needed for **victory over sin.** This power is not of ourselves. Romans 8:9. This involves more than simple control of our actions. It touches every aspect of our lives. It is clearly demonstrated through the fruit of the Spirit, love, joy, patience, kindness, goodness, faithfulness, gentleness, and self-control. Galatians 5:22-3. It is interesting to note how closely this list resembles Paul's description of how love behaves in I Cor. 13:4-6. This is a critical need in our lives. Unfortunately, as important as it is, it is often emphasized to the exclusion of the other two areas of need for power. The result may be a caricature of the grace of God, for it prepares a person for action and then gives him nothing to do.

The **power of the Holy Spirit** is needed corporately to **enable the Church to work together.** John 17:23. This need was a significant part of the Apostle Paul's prayer for the Ephesians.

> I pray that out of his glorious riches he may strengthen you with power <u>through his Spirit</u> in your inner being, so that Christ may dwell in your heart through faith. And I pray that you, being rooted and established in <u>love</u>, may have power, together with all the saints, to grasp how wide and long and high and deep is the <u>love</u> of Christ, and to know this love that surpasses knowledge – that you may be filled to the measure of all the fullness of God (Eph. 3:15-19)

The importance of this prayer becomes clear, when we see the task of the Church, as Paul outlined it, when we see the antagonistic groups of persons who "are being built together to become a dwelling in which God lives by His Spirit" (Eph. 2:22), and when we see the call for unity as expressed in Ephesians 4. If all of this were to be accomplished in the Church then, or now, it is utterly inescapable that we must have the Spirit in all of His power enabling immeasurable love for its accomplishment. We desperately need this love for one another that is deep enough that is surpasses knowledge that Paul describes here in Ephesians 4.

Additionally the **power of the Holy Spirit** is needed both personally and corporately to **effectively witness to the world**. Acts 1:8.

Christ's mission to the world is not dependent on our skilled activities in trying to change people. It is completely dependent on His secret activity in and through His body when and as they are completely found in Him, and He in them. Reaching people is not primarily a matter of words and activity as it is His presence in and through His people as they live a life of obedience to his instructions.

Power for victory over sin and power to enable the church to work together in harmony, are each building blocks for the third. **The power of the Holy Spirit is needed both personally and corporately for power to witness to the world.** God can never be satisfied if only the first two are accomplished.

The Sheppard of the flock left the 99 to go search for the one that was lost. Jesus did not come for the righteous. He came to seek and to save the lost. God sent His only Son Jesus Christ to live and die that all might have salvation. Thus when we are content with, and emphasize only the peace and purity of the church, and fail to emphasize and **appropriate the power of the Holy Spirit to witness**, we show contempt for Jesus Christ and His sacrificial death for all people.

"When the Church has power, the world gets intrigued.

When the Church has power, the world gets convicted.

When the Church has power, the world gets converted.

But no man can be the author of this, though one cannot but feel that tens of thousands of people praying for it and letting themselves be part of the channel of it would give the Holy Spirit the agents that He must want.

Let us pray deeply and often with this little ladder of affirmation and commitment:

> I need the Holy Spirit
> I want the Holy Spirit
> I pray for the Holy Spirit
> I wait for the Holy Spirit."

Shoemaker, Samuel M. With the Holy Spirit and with Fire. Waco TX: Word Books, Rep., 1960

We need then this continual reminder; the Holy Spirit is not present in us for only our personal privilege and pleasure, but also that Christ may touch a lost world through us.

Sometimes this power is needed to open our mouths, probably most of the time it is needed to keep our mouth shut.

Discussion Questions:

Assume: you are God. You are invisible, your prized creation, made in your likeness is estranged and no longer recognizes you. How would you get him back?

You have become a man yourself; have paid the price for man's redemption and reconciliation. Now how would you make yourself known?

How does the plan Christ reveals to His disciples in John 14-17 play out in this?

If Christ intends to be actually present in the world today through the believer, what implication does this have if people only profess to follow Christ, but won't allow Him to guide and control their lives?

What implication does it have if they so separate themselves in their own little world of other believers such that they have no meaningful contact with unbelievers?

What is the real value of the filling of the Holy Spirit? How important is it?

Why?

The Gifts

Gifts are given by God for the accomplishment of the work which he in his wisdom has prepared in advance for us to do. However we make a great mistake if we are only fascinated by the gifts, rather than the Gift of the Holy Spirit who is the giver of all good gifts.

The greatest significance of the gifts is that they are God's method of equipping His people for the specific service they are to render. When we look at gifts given for specific areas of service, we should immediately recognize the link between the Church as a servant and the Church as the body of Christ. Gifts are given in the Church in order that the Church, through its various members may serve effectively in the **whole** of the task that has been given them.

What are Spiritual Gifts? How and when do we receive Spiritual gifts? Spiritual gifts are often thought of in terms of "Christmas gifts" or something given to persons for their use and enjoyment, which are totally separate from their person or personality. While there may be exceptional times when the Spirit bestows a gift for a particular need that is separate from the person he has already created us to be; it does not appear either from scripture or experience that God normally operates this way. God's normal method is to work through those natural talents that he has already given us, and which he shapes as we fully surrender to Him.

Problems arise any time gifts are misunderstood or worse yet misused. In our day of scientific achievement and mindset, it is easy to not expect or accept anything that we cannot explain, and consequently discredit spiritual gifts entirely. It is easy to simply assume that because a person has a given natural ability, that it may directly transfer to spiritual activity. Yet natural ability minus the enabling of God's Spirit is woefully inadequate.

We can also easily have a misplaced valuation of the various gifts. We may highly exalt for example, a speaking gift, while ignore someone who obviously has a gift of discernment, or the gift of hospitality in relating to unbelievers. Worst of all is a tendency to divorce spiritual gifts from the cross.

The fact that there are gifts is a call for both specialization, and cooperation in the life of a local congregation. The congregation needs to recognize and value both the gifts that their pastor has and appreciate his work accordingly. It needs to also recognize areas where there is lack of giftedness and seek giftedness in others to complement those already present. Pastors need to be aware of their own gifts and lack of gifts. They need to value these gifts in others, as a means of enlarging their own, rather than as a threat to their leadership and value in the kingdom.

Pastors need to recognize giftedness among their congregation, both related to interchurch ministries, as well as outwardly focused ministries. All of our teaching, training, equipping, needs to utilize these gifts. We need to identify those areas where we need gifts. While we must avoid seeking gifts in the absence of the Spirit, we must at the same time warmly embrace the gifts God bestows, and the methods through which the Holy Spirit may wish to work.

The Gifts and love

"If I speak in the tongues of men and of angels, but have not love, I am only a resounding gong or a clanging cymbal. If I have a gift of prophecy and can fathom all mysteries and all knowledge, and if I have a faith that can move mountains, but have not love, I am nothing. If I give all I possess to the poor and surrender my body to the flames, but I have not love, I gain nothing. I cor. 13:1-3

In this Scripture the apostle Paul graphically portrays the single greatest problem regarding spiritual gifts, both then and now. So called spiritual gifts exercised in pride and in the absence of sacrificial love are totally ineffective and unfruitful. The Church needs to be continually reminded of some things which ought to be obvious. **One of these is that the absence of love is evidence of the absence of the Spirit of God, since "God is Love" (I John 4:16)** Second, we need to remind ourselves that in the absence of the Spirit of God we can "bear no fruit", we cannot accomplish anything of lasting value.

The continuing truth and urgency of Paul's words to the Corinthian church for today is shockingly brought home by the experience of Charles D. Cooper who spent two weeks on skid row in Detroit as part of his graduate studies. He states:

> During that time not one ministry or agency-related person looked me in the eyes, talked to me directly, inquired specifically or generally of my situation, laughed with me, or touched me. On the other hand, what startled me was the kindness and acceptance I found among street walkers, pushers, pimps, bums, alcoholics, and hustlers.
>
> Upon returning home it took me a great deal of time to diffuse all of my anger I felt as I was consistently 'shunned' by ministry and agency persons -
>
> Charles D. Copper, "Two weeks on Skid Row," The Wesleyan Advocate (Marion, IN.: Wesley Press Jan. 3, 1983) P. 12

Or consider the following incident of a man we will call Sam.

Sam had attended Church all his life, and while on occasion stumbling and falling more openly than some, had endeavored to be a sincere follower of Christ throughout his life. During this time he lost 3 wives to divorce, at least two, in part to the fact, that he and his first wife, had two, handicapped children, with whom these later wives could not cope. These children died in young adulthood. During this time an infant grandchild also died. In spite of faithful attendance and involvement, at many critical times the family was largely ignored by the church they were a part of. The grandchild's death itself triggered anger with God, along with the accompanying erosion of faith. Following the death of the last child, unexpectedly his fourth wife of many years announced that even though he was a nice guy, she no long wanted to be married and wanted a divorce". During this time he also received word that a close relative had died in an accident.

Fortunately, about a year earlier he had chosen to begin attending a different church where he was part of a devout men's *Bible* study group. When he was finally able to share what was happening in his life, these men surrounded him in prayer and support. At one point they laid hands on him in prayer. Following this the group led him to specific resources he needed to deal with his struggles. He later reported: this is the first time in my life that I have had this kind of support. He was over whelmed with gratitude. Why not earlier in his life?

Here we observe both the good and the bad in the ministry of the Church.

Knowing something of the background this writer suspects that in each incident there were those in contact, who believed they were spirit filled. What was the key to failure in effective ministry? Was there judgment that did not allow grace to be given? Was there lack of receptivity that did not allow grace to be received?

Was there failure to equip for ministry, fear of involvement, insensitivity to need? Were there no gifts for ministry, or was there outright hypocrisy? We could ask all these same questions in reverse in regard to the effective ministry.

This incident relates to ministry within the church circle, but it extends well beyond it to a breakdown of effective ministry to unbelievers. Some questioned whether the fourth wife ever came to saving faith. Certainly there was a breakdown in her faith, and a failure of the church to demonstrate clearly the love of Christ to her unbelieving children. It thus illustrates what often happens within our circle of influence outside the Church. It also illustrates what can happen through the influence that comes as we impact in a positive way those within the church and that influence spreads to those same areas of influence outside the Church.

It is here on the level of our interaction with real people that the reality of our Christian experience is tested. It is here that we shall determine whether we will have a ministry to the whole person or whether we will simply go through the motions of church. *The difference is whether one is motivated by love poured into the heart by the Holy Spirit (Rom. 5:5), and working in the power Spirit, and through the gifts that have been given by the same Spirit, or whether in the strength of the flesh and motivated by lesser impulses one uses his own natural abilities to achieve some social goal.*

Discussion Questions:

Salvation cannot be earned. It is not of works lest any should boast. However, behavior was noted by Christ as an issue related to entrance to heaven. What are the character traits of one who has genuine and enduring faith?

Do you feel equipped for ministry to those with whom God has allowed you to be in contact? Why? Why Not? In what areas do you feel that you are clearly lacking and would desire to be equipped for ministry?

What part have others played in equipping you for ministry among the unbeliever's with whom you have daily contact? What part have you played in equipping others for this role?

What part do you believe being equipped or unequipped played a part in the Cooper scenario, the experience Sam had? What would happen in your Church?

What part does our selfish preoccupation and satisfaction with "knowing we are saved", our contentment with having the" blessings of God"; have with the failures of the body of Christ in ministering to itself and the world around it?

I.E. is it possible that we are often so satisfied with the gifts of God including His grace, that we have little heart for what is closest to the heart of God? Are you sensing that God may be prompting you, if so, to what is he prompting you?

Ministry outside the Body

We have been attempting to understand precisely what the bible teaches us about the body of Christ and how Jesus Christ himself set about to bring "lost sheep" into the fold. Here we begin to focus directly on the ministry of the body of Christ in the "world" outside of the activities that are within the confines of the local church. What do the scripture say, or imply related to ministry specifically outside the body of Christ? While this is everyone's ministry, including the pastor who is also responsible for those God places in his sphere of influence, his neighbor, etc.; it is primarily the domain of the laity, whose lives and work naturally place them in this context.

We have been specifically studying the person and ministry of the Holy Spirit in relation to the body of Christ. We have seen that His power and presence in the life of the believer is indispensable to bearing fruit.

Yet across the Church, even among groups where a dominant emphasis is on holiness of life and Spirit filled living, often there is not the accompanying growth of the Church. Donald A McGavran, who is often referred to as the father of the church growth movement, makes a statement which is shocking, yet ought not to surprise us.

"I knew perfectly well that church growth is dependent on the action of the

> Holy Spirit, but since God works in orderly ways and, according to the Scriptures, does not want any to perish, I believed that the Holy Spirit wanted more growth than we were getting. I came to believe that non-growth is a disease, but a curable disease.

I came increasingly to believe that God wanted more growth than we were getting and that if we would go about Christian mission in an enlightened way, God would grant us more growth."
McGavran, Donald A and Hunter, George G. III Church Growth Strategies that Work. Nashville: Abingdon, 1980

Is McGavran wrong, and God does not want, or is powerless to see anymore saved than are being saved? Is it possible that the Church is already fully cooperative, that it fully understands how and where God wants it to work, and that all the possible people that could be saved are being saved? In light of the Scripture and history, these two considerations are untenable. God has specifically declared that He is not willing that any should perish, but that all come to repentance. At Pentecost alone he demonstrated his power to bring thousands to himself in days.

We are forced then to conclude then, that even among those who seek and profess godliness and a Spirit filled life, many believers are unenlightened, not fully cooperating, or for other reasons failing to do what the Spirit wants, and for these reasons persons are not being saved who otherwise would be. This writer believes that at least part of the fault lies with a major flaw in the thinking of the church, starting with the clergy, **who often view the laity as ministry assistance, where everything is focused in an around the local church.** Thus most lay ministries are focused as intra church ministries, and all the training and equipping are focused on these needs. **There needs to be a revolutionary change of focus.** While recognizing the need for these ministries, we must realizes that the **primary place of ministry of the lay person is out where they live every day of their lives and that we need to retool and train and equip them for this very ministry.** This writer believes that when this happens all the other ministries will take on increased vitality and focus.

Fortunately, by the grace of God many Christ followers instinctively understand their role. They fulfill their role out of the love God has given them both for Himself and for their neighbor. In spite of lack of training, or because of inadvertent training, they go about their lives bearing fruit. Because of them the work often goes on in spite of us pastors.

As part of the body of Christ then, we must first seek to be fully cooperating with the Holy Spirit. Second, we need to constantly be listening, and seeking to be fully enlightened, "making the most of every opportunity, because the days are evil" (Eph. 5:16). Third, we need to keep focused on the need for; and actually equipping for, our ministries in and to the "world".

Occupation and Vocation

I overheard a conversion story being excitedly shared a few of years ago at a gathering following a funeral. The story that emerged is summarized as follows:

Two young men in the late 60's were high school teachers. Will call one Art, the other Bill. Art was in Auto shop. Bill was in machine shop. Each had a strong interest in antique autos. They soon became close friends. Restoration including installation of new wood in 30's vehicles and trips to major national antique car swap meets was all part of their activities. These trips included their children and crowding together in one motel room to save money.

The friendship involved not only time spent together but times when Art declined invitations to events in which, he felt he could not participate. Over time Art spent a great deal of time listening to his friend. He knew for example of the abusive relationship Bill had with his dad, in which his dad would beat him "just for kicks."

Over many years the time came when Bill began to treat his own sons in the manner he had been treated. The family was involved in court and Art was asked by Bills wife for help. A letter written to the judge was helpful in keeping the family together but also in remedying the abuse.

40 plus years later they are still friends and Art needs help with a car project and at 1 in the morning they cannot get a bolt in and Art begins to pray aloud "Lord we need help". This lead to a conversation in which Art shared

that he had asked Jesus into his heart at age 18. Bill indicated that nothing like that had been a part of his life.

Months later Bill called to say he had invited Jesus into his heart. That was what all the excited story was about, after over 40 years he now not only has a friend but a brother in Christ to spend eternity with.

The average working adult spends the greatest part of their productive day with non- relatives, many of them are persons with whom they do or can become very well acquainted, often in a very personal way; Because of these opportunities, God calls and gifts persons for a great variety of occupations. These occupations may become the arena of our vocational calling. **Worldly institutions may well train us for our occupation, but it lies with the Church to equip persons for their vocational calling from God.** *For the Christ follower, an occupation ought not to be simply a way to make a living, rather it ought to be a means of being in the right place at the right time to accomplish what God wants whether in the work itself, or for the influence God can give through their life.*

Repeatedly, as I have had contact with young men across the Church, who have become serious about their role in ministry; the immediate response is to begin to think maybe they are called to pastoral ministry. The assumption is that then they could do more, in other words it is seen as the only avenue to really be effective in reaching people. If God is calling them to pastoral ministry, by all means regardless of the difficulty they need to respond, but how tragic, if the call to ministry is within a different occupation where perhaps they could be a community changer, or even a nation changer in God's hands.

When Jesus envisioned His spirit indwelling the believer, this writer does not believe he envisioned Himself only in the calling to the pulpit. Rather, that Jesus saw himself building houses, repairing old ones, making shoes and selling them. He saw Himself in education all the way from preschool to the university. He saw himself in media speaking the truth in love. He saw himself in law enforcement, and criminal justice ensuring that there was in fact justice, for the rich and the poor. Justice for all peoples that was color blind both in theory and in action. He saw Himself in the medical profession, all the way from housekeeping to the highest skill levels possible, bringing about healing not only through medical treatment, but also through faith that heals beginning with the broken human spirit.

He saw Himself in government all the way from Podunk Hollow to the major league. Speaking of major league, yes, he envisioned being in sports as well.

The success or failure of the battles of faith which are fought here will determine the outcome of the decision of millions, even billions of people on the question of faith in Jesus Christ. <u>We can and will truly demonstrate the qualities of "salt" and "light" only when we exercise our ministry through our occupation.</u>

We believe that God not only created this world, but that He also sustains it, that He is interested in the minutest details. He has expressed himself concerning His will in how we treat persons, so he obviously has a will for the way we treat every human being, and the way we meet every circumstance. There is nothing too small to call to God's attention.

We are to exercise our ministry on several levels. First is **the level of the work itself.** All work is to be done such that God is glorified. If He is not lifted up before our fellowmen as good, holy, powerful, loving, just, etc., no one would be drawn to Him. So our work itself ought to draw attention to the glory of God and his work in us. "serve wholeheartedly, as if you were serving the Lord, not men, because you know that the Lord will reward everyone for whatever good he does, whether slave or free" (Eph. 6:7-8)

We should also exercise our **ministry through our occupation,** through a loving Christian presence. There should be both, a natural as well as intentional and habitual intent to be with people, to identify with them, to share in their struggles, and to rejoice in their blessings.

In our occupations, most people do not need to make any special attempt to be with people. Our jobs bring us together every workday. The challenge to us is to let Christ naturally live through us, so that people are positively impacted by the gospel. I recall an incident that happened when I was a student working my way through college in preparation for ministry. One night, I along with 4-5 other men was attempting to pull a piece of equipment into position. It moved suddenly and my inner arm wrapped around a hot steam pipe, curling the flesh. I do not remember much concerning the incident, except the amazement of the others that I did not curse, and trying to answer their questions about why I did not. We cannot program this kind of interaction, but it is a normal part of everyday work.

In section three we will discuss this in greater detail.

A **third level of ministry**, is that of actually communicating the facts of the gospel message. This is an area of ministry that needs to be approached carefully, with great sensitivity to the appropriateness of the time and location, as well as to the person, and to the Holy Spirit. This is often very threatening to sensitive believers. If it is not a bit frightening, maybe you are the kind of person that needs to back off and listen more to God. After all **this is a person** you are dealing with and their eternal destiny may be at stake. Never the less, if you are living a Spirit filled life, those whom God has intended that you speak to; will naturally be in conversation with you over time. Some of these conversations will be about things that matter a great deal to the unbeliever.

I was volunteering to assist in the installation of a new leach line on an existing septic system. We had more time than money. Money was short, so we were hand digging this through clay and shale so we were there for a while. I always try to make people think, often challenging accepted assumptions by asking questions. I was working with two intelligent young men. One had been through a Christian high school, but made no real pretense of faith. The other had attended church 3 times in his life, was raised in a home extremely antagonistic to Christianity. I raised various point regarding Christianity, questions surrounding Christ Himself, and pointed out that Christ himself said to let the tares grow with the wheat; that not everyone who said "Lord, Lord" would enter the kingdom. In other words I was lifting up Christ and attempting to distinguish between

Christ and some of the negative aspects of the Church. We discussed everything from the value of work to, having a meaningful purpose in life and beyond. This went on for 3 days. I had known these young men most of their lives. I was seriously interested in them and so much of the time I was seriously digging for what these young men thought and valued. I really wanted to know, and I spent considerable time listening. Over the 3 days I could sense a change in attitude. With this change of attitude I thought it would be appropriate to invite them to church the next Sunday. I did, they accepted. Joe Indicated that It was the first he had ever attend church where it ever made any sense.

A couple of months passed and I was back helping to finish the job which they had progressed with while I was gone. I was pleased and surprised by a complete change of attitude, and the thought through conclusions, of Joe who had the almost nonexistent, but negative Christian background. I finally questioned Joe carefully as to whether; he had come to faith in Christ. He indicated that he had.

During our normal activities over time, questions may arise; you may ask questions, honest answers will be given with Godly wisdom. In bits and pieces, perhaps over years, the word will be shared. God is patient, we need to be also. As the word takes root, and spiritual hunger is shown, God can use you, another Christian friend, or a church service, but God will lead if given opportunity. Again, more on this in section three.

There is yet a **fourth level of ministry** for the laity in the sphere of the world. This ministry intersects with all the others. This is the area of addressing the social needs and evils of society in broad ways that require the involvement of large numbers of people working together. Jesus did in fact teach us to pray, "your kingdom come, your will be done on earth as it is in heaven." This cannot happen if we are not involved in our communities doing what is his will for us to do. Slavery ended in the U. S. at least in part because of this kind of ministry. This in spite of the fact that even as this was happening there were those so blinded by prejudice within the Church itself, that they not only held slaves, but defended it.

The Church requires great clarity and sacrificial love if these needs are to be properly addressed. It is easy to think we are ministering, as in the Cooper example on Skid Row, while in fact avoiding any real love of individuals. It is very easy to condemn and hate the sinner, in the name of hating the sin. God forbid, yet at present the Bible thumping Evangelical church in America is better known, in many instances, on the news, for some of its hate than it is for its compassion. This creates a negative image with many unbelievers that is remembered and must be processed if they are too seriously face and evaluate the claims of Jesus Christ.

Addressing social needs, need not necessarily be a call for organized participation, but it does require great numbers of the body of Christ working together as "salt" and "light" penetrating the community in which they live. This type of ministry may, or may not, not directly affect evangelism; however it always when done in sacrificial love, assists in creating a climate wherein evangelism can be nourished.

Webs of Relationship

In the early 1930's Donald A McGavran first began to discover the principle of webs of relationship as a powerful factor in church growth. This principle may be stated as follows:

"The faith spreads most naturally and contagiously along the lines of the social network of living Christians, <u>especially new Christians</u>. Receptive undiscipled men and women usually receive the possibility when the invitation is extended to them from credible Christian friends, relatives, neighbors, and fellow workers from within their social web". McGavran and Hunter, Growth Strategies, P.30

Church growth through webs of relationship is well illustrated by the great growth of a church in Taiwan. The growth "began when the pastor, the Reverend Lee, visited in the hospital a Mr. Hwang, who accepted the Christian faith and asked for and received baptism, and shortly died. Lee led the funeral service where many relatives and friends of Mr. Hwang gathered. The widow, Mrs. Hwang and her children soon became Christians. A close friend attended the funeral; he and his whole family became converts. Another close friend attended the funeral, Lee visited him; he became a Christian and proceeded to evangelize the other members of his family. One evening as he told Bible stories to his children, his own grandmother overheard the stories. There came a stirring in her depths; she became a Christian and led another grandson and a neighbor woman into the faith. That neighbor led her husband, a policeman, into the faith, who in turn evangelized his police beat partner. That second policeman led his wife, who in turn led a neighbor, who in turn let her husband and daughter, into the Christian faith, and the daughter's husband came in too, and on and on". Ibid

Out of just this single web of relationships came a mighty growing congregation in Taiwan.

This dramatizes the effects of people following the natural relationships in sharing the Christian faith. It also focuses on the need and effectiveness of person to person ministry outside the four walls of the church. It tells us that people of all walks of life, regardless of age can be used of God to share their faith.

In my own experience, I was mentoring a young man who was saved while in jail. He was eager for the word and I met with him weekly for over 2 years after he was out. We seriously discussed virtually every topic a young man with no real parenting would be concerned with. He faced issues that brought a long disconnect. When he finally sought me out again, I discovered that though he was participating in a questionable lifestyle, a lifestyle he was attempting to break free of, his faith still was real, and he had led his girlfriend to faith in Christ. All of this happened within a culture that has been very difficult for the Church to penetrate. Yet it was a natural connection for him and thus the gospel could cross barriers otherwise impenetrable.

Awareness of the importance of webs of relationship allows us to look at the New Testament Church with fresh insight. What does a study of the New Testament reveal in this regard?

During earlier study, I was focused on the Book of Acts, in later studies; I realized there were examples even earlier than that. Luke records, Jesus calling of Peter and Andrew, James and John. Seed was sown over a period of time, but it appears they came to decisions of faith largely as a group. (Luke 5:1-11) There was a social network of which Jesus was a part, hence his casual use of their boats and his encouragement after his sermon to "Put out into the deep water and let down their nets for a catch", when he knew they were tired and discouraged by their earlier efforts.

John 4 records Jesus dialogue and interaction with the woman at the well. Jesus uses unashamed lack of prejudice, and curiosity to give opening to speak to this woman. The conversation leads to her coming to faith in Him as the Messiah. This in itself, is great and lends itself as a great training tool in understanding how to reach people. But note what follows: "Many of the Samaritans from the town believed in him because of the woman's testimony, 'He told me everything I ever did.' So when the Samaritans came to him, they urged him to stay with them, and he stayed two days. And because of his words many more became believers. (John 4:39-41)

Luke records several incidences in the book of Acts. The first incident gives probable evidence: At the time when the number of disciples was increasing, the Grecian Jew complained against the Aramaic-speaking community (Acts 6:2). This represents two probable webs of relationship. Again, a man from Lydda named Aeneas was healed. "All those who lived in Lydda and Sharon saw him and turned to the Lord" (Acts 9:35)

Other examples abound as we look at Households such as that of Cornelius, and the Philippian jailor. The following is an especially clear example:

> Now those who had been scattered by the persecution in connection with Stephen traveled as far as Phoenicia, Cyprus, and Antioch, telling the message only to Jews. Some of them, however, men from Cyprus and Cyrene, went to Antioch and began to speak to Greeks also, telling them the good news about the Lord Jesus. The Lord's hand was with them, and a great number of people believed and turned to the Lord (Act 11:19-21).

The first thing we see here is the gospel spreading through the web of relationships among the Jews. Most persons did not share the gospel beyond these boundaries. However, some men from Cyprus and Cyrene crossed over a bridge, perhaps a bridge of friendship resulting from their occupation. These men shared the gospel with a new group of people, the Greeks. Some of these believed and the gospel began to spread among this new people in their web of relationships.

Building Bridges

When the apostle Paul when on his missionary journeys, he had two primary target audiences. He preached first to the Jews, then to the Gentiles. However it is especially important to take note of who these Gentiles were. They were not just any Gentile he could find. Typically, as at Thessalonica, they were Godfearers from the various peoples of the earth. In other words they were people who already were responsive to God. They were person who already had contact with the Jews religiously. Significantly, they already also had contact with their own people ethnically. Among these people we discover many of the first Gentile converts to the Christian faith. This is strategically important. Remember Paul was being led by the Holy Spirit! Paul was preaching to persons who were both on the "bridge", and were themselves, yet another bridge to new groups of people.

Gospel bridges are the contact over which the gospel flows between persons, and different groups of people. At times people themselves are the bridges. At other times the bridges are formed by the social contacts between people. Some bridges come about naturally, as through occupational contact; others may be formed artificially by a deliberate involvement for example in an organization.

Natural bridges are created by the normal social contacts between persons of the homogeneous unit. These contacts may come in various ways. They may come through the interaction of persons with their own people in community life, occupation, or family gatherings. They may come as persons deliberately attempt to be sensitive to the needs of persons in their own social unit. They may also be created by persons who are themselves "bridges". Persons are natural bridges when because of their occupation, community involvement, or other natural factors they have sufficient natural contacts to form a bridge over which the gospel can flow between two differing homogeneous units.

Artificial bridges are created by the social contacts between persons who are of different homogeneous units, and who have no means of contact without creating them. Contacts may be created through deliberate ministry to the needs among the target population; this usually requires much time and effort. If a local Church has lost its contact, it should use all means possible to build bridges. These contacts may come more naturally, as persons deliberately place themselves within target populations through occupation or housing. However the importance of the ministry of the laity is underscored as we consider all of the places God has already placed them.

How important are bridges to the spread of the gospel? Where and when do we need to build bridges over which the gospel can pass? Are there situations in which we ought not to concentrate on building bridges?

Most people stay in their comfort zone. Even forcing them out is usually difficult. Whereas people will try new things if a friend goes with them. The same is true in introducing a person to Jesus Christ. In fact, <u>if significant social or cultural barriers must be crossed, only small numbers of persons from that homogeneous unit of people will become Christians.</u> This highlights the importance of bridges over which the gospel can pass. Ways must be found for the gospel to pass <u>to</u> people, rather than <u>forcing people to cross</u> unnecessary barriers to receive the gospel. Ministry of person to person contact, within our daily work often give us a natural bridge to people very different to us who then already have contact with others of their own people.

Obviously if there are already bridges in place we ought not to waste time building them. On the other hand, if in the area of our ministry there are no bridges available to a people groups, we need by all means build them. However, it is most important that we observe where God is already working. This is a critical area where the body of Christ, with its feet already on the ground, its hands already busy, its eyes open, its ears listening, can become aware of responsive persons and groups of persons around them.

If in fact bridges do need to be built, the current trend of "outward focus" is timely. There are all kinds of social needs in our communities that can bring about meaningful contacts with in target groups of lost people. We need not even start an organization, often we can partner individually or as groups with groups already in existence. In so doing we may even be able to bring about greater unity within the Church.

In looking at this subject we must take seriously the fact that the world is made up of a mosaic of many different homogeneous units of people. In the industrialized west, any one metropolitan area may be made up of many very separate social units. In America we may refer to ourselves as a melting pot and while in a sense we are, on the other hand, we are made up of many, many people groups, wherein its members socialize and inter-marry very largely within their own confines, and often become in their own minds a separate race. In other instances they may be set apart by their different values, leisure time, occupations, expectations of life, or even their expectation of Church.

More bridges are needed whenever there is a unit of people within which there are no or few persons who can effectively reach and teach their own people. In these situations in is necessary for someone to cross cultural and social barriers for these persons to become Christians. We need to use Godly wisdom it this. Bridges need to be built without requiring them to follow us back across the bridge. In other words, we must build a beach head where they can come together around the word and Christ in their own world and culture.

Discussion Questions:

On what levels are you currently engaged in ministry? On what level is your local Church engaged in ministry?

Are you meaningfully engaged with unbelievers around you? Is your local Church? Jesus was a friend of Sinners. Have you acted as a friend, such that some of them would consider you a true friend?

Do you? Does your church need to find areas of community involvement that will allow you to build bridges to those in your community?

Are their people groups around you, to whom if there were a bridge built, might come quickly as a group to Christ? If so what priority, what sacrifice would Christ have us make to make this possible?

Do we really believe that all the people whom God wants to be saved are being saved, or might there be others whom God longs for who would respond if we acted wisely, with sacrificial love?

Is it possible that some who seem so uninterested, so focused on sinful pleasure, would in fact turn to Christ if the "light" were turned on, if they really saw Christ in His love living among them?

If so what would that love, that light look like in contrast to charity and my own human insights?

Can God give us these answers if we truly seek him individually and as groups for these answers as we pray?

Summary of Section I

God has been attempting to reveal Himself to man ever since man's separation from himself through sin. The existence of God is obvious through His creation. Were man not blinded by the sin, much could be known that is not perceived. In the midst of this God has sought to make Himself known through a physical presence and visible example, first through Israel, second through His Son, now through his body, the Church.

Man departed from God through unbelief. The way back to God has always required a return to faith demonstrated through obedience to God's instructions. Abraham was such a man of faith. He demonstrates through his life not only the fact of such faith, but also the struggle to achieve and maintain this faith.

God chose Abraham with a purpose. He promised Abraham, "all peoples on earth will be blessed through you" Gen. 12:3b. He promised Abraham, "I will make you into a great nation" Gen. 12:2. God continued to choose this nation, not because they were anything special but because in spite of their stiff necked rebellion, he continued to have the overwhelming purpose of bringing salvation to all peoples.

Much is made of God's choosing. I believe that we often fail to give proper consideration for **why God chooses.** Israel arrogantly misunderstood God choice of them as a nation, ignoring the purpose for which they were chosen, as a result those of Israel whom God foreknew would not trust Him were rejected of God because of their unbelief. God continues to choose those who will respond to Him by faith, and thus attain the righteousness that is attained only by faith.

Because of unbelief, the visible Church is in great danger in this regard. The Church is God's chosen vessel to be his presence in the world today. However, the apostle Paul makes clear in Romans 11 that If God did not spare the natural branches (Israel) because of their unbelief, He surely will not spare those grafted in to the vine if they persist in unbelief. Imperfections have been, are, and will always be a part of the Church, and thus require the grace of God, but only those who are being made righteous through a continuing relationship of faith are and will continue to be part of the true invisible Church. Even though they may be part of the visible Church and active in doing good deeds, they are no longer his Servant, his hands, His feet, His eyes, His ears, His mouth, making His presence, His love known in the darkness of this world.

In Mathew 25 Jesus pictures caring for the hungry and thirsty of this world as one example of what a genuine relationship of faith looks like. It is not a recipe for what we have to do to be saved. We are never saved by our good works or lost for our lack of them. But when faith is real, it results in a genuine relationship with Jesus Christ, good works will then be a result as we respond to his Spirit in obedience. That obedience will always require involvement with the people whom God places around us. For many you may be the one person God can use. This usefulness will not likely come at some point where you consciously make an effort, but rather through the daily practice of letting Christ live in and through you, and at a moment of which you are unaware.

The body of Christ is made up of persons of such a wide kaleidoscope of personalities, cultures, temperaments, styles of worship, perspectives on life itself, and on theology; that from a human standpoint Unity seems impossible. Yet, "in Christ" and with "Christ in us" unity is very possible where and when we center on those truths that are most clearly taught and which are the essence of the Christian faith. It is not only possible, but essential if we are to demonstrate the reality of Christ in us, as the only hope of a searching world.

This unity becomes possible and practical when we each respond with obedience and love to Christ as our Head; we live in listening obedience to Christ, not just as Savior, but as Lord of our lives.

We are not looking for structural unity, or for unity just for the sake of convenience. We are not looking for commonality or sameness. We are looking for shared life and purpose as we dwell in Christ and he is truly present in us and the diverse persons whom He has created, working out His life among them.

This life will be expressed uniquely as each use the gifts and talents that God has given them. I think of Joseph, a karate instructor, extravert, electrical engineer, excited about Christ, talking to people, making friends wherever he goes. I think of Edwin, education administrator, quiet but friendly, thoughtful, analytical, a leader without destroying others in doing so. I think of Dave and Phyllis, retired yet still constantly involved in their community, touching people, praying and responding to needs around them, living out their faith. God can and does use each uniquely. Such persons can compete, or in yielding to the leadership of God's Spirit, can become a unique team. The real question is will such persons humble themselves to a role of submission to God, listen to His voice, respond in obedience, let Christ truly be formed within them such that there is unity and effective ministry.

God has placed Joseph and Edwin's, Dave and Phyllis's all over this planet, in every strata of life, every metropolis, every hamlet, and every occupation where faith is possible. He wants to see them equipped and discipled to live out His life right where they are, so that everyone will have opportunity to believe.

Section Two

A Christ followers interaction with Christ

Interaction with Christ; The absolute foundation for all other interactions of a Christ follower.

I invite you at this point to join me as we begin specifically to identify what you and I must do and be, to play our part in fulfilling the mission God wishes to accomplish through us.

We will attempt to be both biblical, and practical: to see both the function of the body Christ and our function as individuals. There are four essential ingredients involved in our interaction with Christ. They are summarized here. First, we must dwell in Christ. This not only is first in time, it is first in importance. It is absolutely essential to all the others. We cannot "bear fruit unless we dwell in the vine". Second, we must learn to listen to God. If we cannot, or do not hear His voice, we cannot do what he tells us to do. Third, we must obey God. Without obedience, at best our life in Christ cannot go forward, at worst we are cut off from the vine. Fourth, we must receive grace. God has good works that he has prepared for us to do, however we all stumble and fall in ignorance and weakness. Constant new grace is required for us to go forward. This grace enables us to dwell in Him, and the cycle is allowed to continue.

A. Dwelling in Christ

It is my intention to look at dwelling in Jesus Christ from a different perspective than you may be accustomed to. It will be different at least from the writers whom I have read. **We are looking at it from the vantage point of the mission of Jesus Christ.** Many other devotional writers have done an excellent job of describing what it means to have that privilege of going deep in our relationship with God. There is certainly nothing in itself that is bad about going deep with God. **However, we miss the point of an abiding relationship with God, if we think that it is only for our self, and fail to understand that it is also a missional relationship.** If we think that dwelling in Christ is only for us, we may not only be ineffective in ways God wants to use us, but also fail in our efforts to draw near to God because we are living an unhealthy spiritual lifestyle. God means for us to exercise as well as eat.

What then does it really mean to dwell in Christ? Translator's use a number of different words, including the following; "remain", "abide", and "live". Each word used by Translators, gives a little different connotation. However each of the words suggest something more than an experience that happens at one point in time. Each suggests an ongoing relationship with Jesus Christ. Each suggests that we are to settle in; we are to be there for the duration. Yet it also suggests that this is a day to day decision. When I chose over 54 years ago to marry my wife, it was a decision for life. Yet it is a decision that by its very nature requires reaffirmation on a regular basis. Abiding or dwelling in Christ also involves these daily choices, without them the first choice can become meaningless.

Given the context of Jesus instruction to us as part of his description of us as branches in a vine, it is clear that it has to be an ongoing relationship for us to be alive at all, let alone bear fruit.

As we search the scriptures attempting to define what the relationship of dwelling in Christ is intended to be, we find several clear guidelines.

1. It is to be a love relationship. We love him because He first loved us.

The whole of the *Bible* teaches us that God takes the initiative in this relationship. Sin has invaded our life so deeply that Ephesians describes us prior to God's intervention as "dead in sin". Because He loves us, God has placed within us the very ability to seek Him, as well as to find Him. Regardless of the theological direction from which you approach, in some manner God's grace goes before us enabling us to respond. You and I however must make a response. We have the opportunity to respond to His love, or reject it.

We always come to God from some position of need, whether at a most basic level of physical need, the level of emotional need, or driven by lack of purpose. Jesus appealed to people at every level.

Note His appeal in the following passage as an example:

Jesus said; "Come unto me, all you who are weary and burdened, and I will give you rest. Take my yoke upon you and learn of me, for I am gentle and humble in heart, and you will find rest for your souls. For my yoke is easy and my burden is light." Matt. 11:28-30

Initially we return love, in exchange for the good we perceive we are receiving, even as a couple, newly acquainted give and receive love in the excitement of first relationship. This love is shallow. It is only in relationship over time and tested by difficulty that mature love develops. A growing relationship takes time. It requires getting acquainted with God on an experiential level. It requires much time in His word getting acquainted with him through what He says about Himself and through seeing him in the experiences of others, both in their good choices, and in their bad choices.

It requires **living in His word**; beginning to practice in His strength what he clearly is telling me in the Word. We must start with the little things, things that may not even appear, at least to others, to really matter. I follow by doing what I intuitively know he is telling me within my spirit as I respond to His Spirit within me. It is in this relationship that I really begin to Know Him. I worship, serve and study with fellow believers. I observe their lives, particularly those who are clearly serious in their commitment to know God. As I begin to see Him as he is and respond to His Spirit within, I will go well beyond a choice to love and trust him, to a love that will not let me go, to where I value Him more highly than anything this world could possibly offer.

The ultimate goal of living, or dwelling in Christ is Christ likeness. We are transformed into His image as we constantly live in Him and He lives in us. This is not simply our goal, it is the predetermined destination of those God foreknows will choose to trust him with their lives. See Romans 8:29. God will graciously use every circumstance of our lives, both good and bad, to bring us to His likeness as we cooperate with Him.

2. It is a relationship between unequals. He is the vine the very source of our life. We are the branches and totally dependent upon Him.

God is in fact, God. Even those who wish to deny this fact, eventually realize if nothing else that they themselves are not God.

As we come to faith in Jesus Christ we come to realize the great privilege that it is for a finite being to live in loving relationship with one who is infinite. Yes, we are as vessels in the hands of the potter. **Yet** Jesus told his disciples:

"I no longer call you servants, because a servant does not know his master business. Instead I have called you friends, for everything I have learned from my Father I have made know to you. You did not choose me, but I chose you and appointed you to go and bear fruit---fruit that will last." John 15:15-16

We the finite have been invited to be <u>friends and partners</u> with the infinite God. What an immense privilege, even as the lowest servant, getting to associate at an intimate level with the Lord of the universe.

3. It is a relationship that is voluntary.

    We are neither forced into it, nor forced to continue. Man was
    created in the very image of God. Foundational to this are the
    characteristics of intelligence, and the ability to choose. Without
    this we would be incapable of love. God does want us to love him.
    Love however, by its very nature is voluntary, it cannot be forced.
    Man in the beginning walked in fellowship with God. When
    confronted with temptation and Choice, he stepped back, looked
    at God, and decided that maybe God was not so good after all.
    He believed the tempter, **disbelieved God**, and chose to disobey.
    God knew this risk, and had planned for it, before the foundations
    of the earth.

    In relation to our thinking processes, there are three words
    inseparable linked, faith, love and obedience. Ever since that first
    act of unbelief and disobedience, God has in relation to time and
    history, been involved in bringing all who were willing back into
    a faith, love, obedience relationship. You cannot fully believe and
    love God, and not attempt to obey Him. God sent His son to this
    earth to live and die to reestablish this love relationship. On our
    part, once we begin to respond in faith to the love God offers, we
    spend the rest our lives trying to understand, taking large and
    small steps, sometimes back and forth, as we learn to trust Him
    (have faith), love Him, and consequently to obey Him.

4. It is a relationship that is costly, but brings joy and vitality to our lives.

    He gave his life to make the relationship possible. He continues to
    graciously give us all things. It is costly for us as well. He requires
    that we trust Him, that we accept his leadership and ruler-ship in
    our lives. He requires that we die to self and live for Him.

    I will not spend time here to detail the cost to God since the story
    of Christ Himself is likely familiar to those reading this, except to
    say; the cost to God was not just to see his only begotten Son die.
    Since God is one, one God in three persons, God fully participated

in the death that took place on Calvary. God did not just send His Son to do the dirty work, God suffered there on the cross, for you, and for me.

What of the cost to us?

First, let's be honest! It is Satan's lie that we should come to God without expectation of reward. However the truth is, none of us do anything without motivation, the expectation of reward. Jesus is our example of willingness to suffer, to give the ultimate sacrifice because of His love for another. He is also the example of rewards that are worth the cost involved.

"Let us fix our eyes on Jesus, the author and perfecter of our faith, *who for the joy set before him* endured the cross, scorning its shame ---- so that you will not lose heart" Hebrews 12:2-3.

What was the "joy set before Jesus"? It was the expectation of a love relationship with the redeemed Children of God. It included the expectation of a love relationship with you and me.

What then is the reward that we reach forward to?

In John 15:11 Jesus set before us the expectation that: His "joy may be in you and that your joy may be complete." Have you ever experienced the joy of a real love relationship with Christ, of walking in obedience that results from wanting to do anything, and everything, that he desires of you? A love relationship with Jesus Christ becomes a reward in itself. If we come to properly understand the nature of this relationship we will see that this is reward like no other. It will be well worth it to sell all we have in order to purchase the field with the buried pearl of great price.

What is the nature of the cost to us?

If we observe the scripture, carefully at this point we will see that cost and reward are inseparably entwined.

Note Jesus words in this regard:

"Whoever finds his life will lose it, and whoever loses his life for my sake will find it" Matt. 10:39 Or again, If anyone would come after me, he must deny himself and take up his cross and follow me. For whoever wants to save his life will lose it, but whoever loses his life for me will find it. What good will it be if a man gains the whole world, yet forfeits his soul? Or what can a man give in exchange for his soul? For the Son of Man is going to come in his Father's glory with his angel, and then he will reward each person according to what he has done." Matt. 16:24-28.

Jesus demands that we surrender our very self to Him. In exchange he gives us our life back in a manner that allows us to live our lives abundantly. Often, he does not change our external circumstances, so much as he changes us and how we react and interact in those same circumstances. Few of us do it, but what would it be like to live our lives completely without fear, or worry? If we always had complete faith and confidence in God, if we always lived in complete obedience we could do just that. God is completely capable of meeting our every need. This is true even to the extent of meeting our need should we face and experience deprivation and death for His sake.

God wants to supply our need, but he calls on us to **die to self** in order that he may accomplish his work through us. The apostle Paul says: "I have been crucified with Christ, and I no longer live, but Christ lives in me. The life I live in the body, I live by faith in the Son of God, who loved me and gave himself for me."

We are called upon to worship God, and show our love by "offering our bodies as living sacrifices, holy, and pleasing to God" Rom. 12:1.

January 8, 1956, 5 missionary men lost their lives, in a swift hail of long, black, wooden lance, in an effort to reach the Auca Indians of Ecuador, with the message of the gospel. These were not young men who accidently stumbled in to unknown danger. They were men who willingly and daily had been placing their lives in the service of their master. From my youth I remember the words of one of them, Jim Elliott, "He is no fool who gives what he cannot keep, to gain that which he cannot lose." More recently I have read the book based on Nate Saints diary, Jungle Pilot, by Russell T. Hitt, in which He discusses "expendability". A veteran of World War II, Nate states: "during the last war we were taught that, in order to obtain our objective, we had to be willing to be expendable, and many lives were spent paying the price of our redemption from the bonds of political slavery.

"This very afternoon thousands of soldiers are known by their serial numbers as men who are expendable. During the last war we saw big bombers on the assembly line, row after row, powerful, costly implements of war! Yet we all knew that many of those bombers would not even accomplish five missions over enemy territory. We also knew that young fellows, many of them volunteers, would ride in those airborne machine-gun turrets, and their life expectancy behind those guns was, with the finger on the trigger down, only *four minutes*. Tremendous expendability! Hitt, Russel T. Jungle Pilot with Epilogue by Steven F. Saint. Grand Rapids, MI: Discovery House Publishers, 1959 Updated 1997

"We know that there is only one answer when our country demands that we share in the price of freedom---yet when the Lord Jesus Christ asks us to pay the price for world evangelism, we often answer without a word. We cannot go. We say it costs too much." Hitt, Jungle Pilot, Ibid

"God Himself laid down the law when He built the universe. He knew when He made it what the price was going to be. And the Lamb of God was slain in the councils of God from before the foundation of the world. If God didn't hold back His only Son, but gave Him up to pay the price for our failure and sin, than how can we Christians hold back our own lives---the lives He really owns?"

"The Lord tells us that He that loveth his life---we might say that he that is selfish with his life---shall lose it. It's inescapable". Hitt, Jungle Pilot. Ibid

Most of us are not called to in fact lose our physical lives for the gospel as were these men, but regardless of our place in the hierarchy of the church, we are called upon by Christ Himself to offer ourselves as "living sacrifices". Hitt, Ibid

Becoming a living sacrifice requires daily decisions that require, the empowering of the Spirit to accomplish, yet it is only as this is what is happening in our lives, that it goes beyond what can happen in the strength of the flesh. <u>When the tenor of what is happening in our lives **requires** the empowering of the Holy Spirit, and our responses are ones empowered by His Spirit, then the world, those around us begin to take notice.</u> Living in our own strength, even with good deeds we may in fact be as unnoticeable an unmarked grave. We may notice all our good deeds done in the flesh. When we are living in the Spirit we may not even be aware of those time in which Jesus is lifted up through our lives. Yes, we can expect difficulty, even persecution, but it may be in this that others around us see a glimpse of who Christ really is.

The picture of an unmarked grave hit me powerfully this morning as I was reading Christ's words in Luke 11:44 "Woe to you, because you are like unmarked graves, which men walk over without ever knowing it." We cannot be salt and light, unless God's Spirit does indeed dwell within. Without it either we are different for all the wrong reasons, or we have no distinctiveness that the world around us pays any attention to. When Christ truly dwells within we are a breath of fresh air, a sweet aroma, light in the darkness.

Jesus tells us to dwell in Him. When we are willing to give up self in order to dwell in him, we will discover over time that we are bearing fruit. First the fruit of His Spirit, "love, joy, peace, patience, kindness, goodness, faithfulness, gentleness, and self-control" Gal. 5:22-23, but also "fruit that will last" John 15:16. We will also see the fruit of contributing to others coming into loving relationship with Christ Himself.

5. It is a relationship that connects us to the very source of life itself. Apart from this relationship we are separate from life in the Spirit itself, and our work losses its value.

The Church is often polarized between what may be referred to as either sloppy grace or legalism. It is not a question of avoiding either extreme. It is a question of remaining, living, abiding in Christ. If we stay in Him, his instructions will guide our lives, His grace will encourage and restore when we fail in ignorance or weakness. His Spirit will discipline and reprove when we stray.

In his book, I Was Wrong, Jim Baker of PTL (Praise the Lord) fame or infamy relates his experiences connected with the fall of PTL, and his subsequent imprisonment. While not ever believing himself to be guilty of intending to defraud, he clearly sees his wrong in many areas of scriptural interpretation and relationships. While from outward appearance it seemed there was much fruit, God took him through what at the very least was an extreme pruning, or discipling process.

"Could it be? I wondered. *Could it possibly be true that I was in prison by the very design of God? Was there really a larger purpose behind my imprisonment, as some of my friends implied?"* Baker, Jim, I was Wrong, Nashville, TN: Thomas Nelson, Inc. 1996 *P. 234,*

"God had been showing me in many ways that the primary reason He had allowed me to be imprisoned was not to punish me, nor was it so I could minister to other prisoners; I was in prison so I could get to know Him." Baker, Ibid P. 294

Jim relates his discovery for example of the difference between Jesus use of the word we translate "know" in Matthew 7:23, in which Jesus is referring to an intimate relationship even as when the bible talks of a man knowing his wife in an intimate relationship; and the example of Peter's use of the word "know" in Matthew 26:74, where the meaning is "to perceive with a physical sight".

"As I reread the passage (Matthew 7:21-23) with that understanding, I realized that Jesus was describing people who would say to Him, 'Jesus, we did powerful things in your name. We had dynamite choirs. I was a dynamite preacher. We built wonderful buildings in your name. We did wonderful works, all in your name.'

Yet Jesus said that He did not know them!" Baker, Ibid P. 463,

Much good work can be done in the strength of the flesh, using human talents; however, separated from the source of life itself that comes from an abiding relationship with Jesus Christ; its value will not last.

6. It is a relationship in which we come to Him with the greatest of weakness, ignorance, and sinfulness, and through his redeeming and life giving power, become strong, full of godly wisdom, gain the righteousness that is by faith; righteousness both in record and in actual change of character. We are ultimately glorified with Him.

Much controversy has and is taking place over what God does, and what man does in the process of salvation. There are several things that are obvious, both by observing man, and through attention to the word. First, is that if God be God in the Christian definition, he is indeed sovereign; he can do anything that he chooses to do. It is not a question of power or ability. It has to do with His nature. It has to do with what he will do, will chose to do given his nature, as a Holy God who can and will do no wrong; a God who is Love, not just a God who loves, but who **is love.** It has to do with what a God will do who is Just, who is just for eternity. The book of Romans deals with clear cut teaching that indicated that none will be saved, or can be saved except through the "righteousness that comes through faith". It also sorts through a considerable "what if" sections in Chapters 9-11, rounding this out with a doxology in 11:33-36 where we are reminded of man's weak understanding in comparison to God wisdom and knowledge. God always treats man better than he deserves. I take comfort in the fact that God knows what he is doing and that his love is such He truly seeks the lost "not wanting any one to perish, but everyone to come to repentance." II Peter 3:

With this reasoning, I believe a second fact is obvious. God truly gives everyone real choices. God lifts or upholds, God takes his hand off and allows perverse behavior, (as in Rom. 1 24.26, 28), God leaves people alone, he convicts of guilt, He allows pain, he takes away pain, but everything is done in love in an effort to bring them back to himself in a love relationship. I noted with interest in this morning's time with God as I read regarding

David and Absalom, "God does not take away life: instead he devises ways so that the banished person, may not remain estranged from Him." II Sam. 14:14. God never simply takes advantage of our weakness to use for his glory, he uses our weakness to bring glory to himself, but in the process gives people an opportunity to seek and find Him and his great love. As people come to see God as He really is (see His glory), then they also begin to see him as a God they can trust and worship.

Third, it is obvious that while God comes to us, lifts us to the point where we can make the choice to believe and be just as if we had never sinned, because of His Son Jesus; He does not stop there. Real righteousness is available to us. Sanctification, holiness, and purity, are not just abstract words in the bible. God means to change our character, and with growing faith and cooperation (choice) on our part he gets started here and now. He changes not only how he perceives us, and our relationship with him; he changes how we relate to our family, in our work place, in our community, and yes even to our church.

Dan and Jill were long time acquaintances of about 10 years. Theirs had always seemed a troubled marriage, getting worse as time went on. Both had a background that gave sketchy information regarding Christ. They had attended church occasionally in a formal setting, without serious commitment, but would have called themselves Christian. There had been a recent period of separation, with conversation with lawyers, followed by reconciliation. I became seriously involved, Traveling through I am asked to have a talk with Eric, a friend of the family, who has broken in to a liquor store and is now in trouble with the law. Because of this incident Dan and Jill were at each other's throats, trying for a death grip. I had not seen Eric in years, he is now 17. What is a retired person going to say that will mean anything, but I have to try? Here is where prior prayer, study of the word, and the leadership of the Spirit make a difference. Nothing that followed resulted from my brilliance or cleverness.

Soon into our conversation, I think to myself. He has broken the law; why not talk to him about the positive side of the law. He was willing so I began to share the positive side of the 10 commandments. Soon he responded, "No wonder my grandfather was all ways reading his bible". I soon realized Eric was open and responsive, so I continued. That day Eric received Christ. I saw Jill the next day at a neighborhood gathering. She immediately cornered me and said, "What did you do to Eric"? I told her what had occurred. She said. "He came home with a completely different attitude, and talked with me the most he has in years"

This set the stage and I knew that I had to talk to Dan and Jill. Again what was I to say? They had already had professional counseling. It was difficult to set up a time and a place, first because Dan did not believe that Jill would be willing to set down anywhere with him, second because schedules were in fact full to the extreme. But we got together about 4 days later. Again, I had to rely on the leadership of the Holy Spirit, and my confidence in what God could do it they would let Him. With trepidation, I waded in with Ephesians 5:21-33, where it starts with "submit to one another out of reference to Christ" I explained that this was one of the biblical models of a healthy marriage. I hit especially hard on the man's role, downplaying about to extinction the man's role as head, and emphasizing how Christ was the role model as one who sacrificed himself to death in order to present himself with a blood washed beautiful bride. We talked, (when I could keep them from arguing) about what that would entail in their daily lives.

I explained that I could not solve their problems, but that Christ could. I asked their willingness to submit themselves to Christ, and then submit to their spouse when and as Christ instructed them to do. We prayed together, and I left. Thank God they listened, and began to submit to Christ. Less than a week later Dan called me all excited. Jill had apologized to him 3-4 times in the last several days, more than he could remember in ten years of marriage. Jill reported, "Something will happen where normally he would be abusive, he will be just standing there. I can tell he is praying."

Dwelling in Christ means living in relation to him in such a way that in Christ I become strong, and he changes me from the inside out, now and for eternity.

7. It is a relationship in which we have a reliable guide for knowing what truth is and how to relate it to the world in which we live.

Jesus said, "I am the way, and **the truth**, and the life" John 14:6. An old quote I remember, perhaps from a sermon states, "I am the way for going, the truth for knowing, and the life for living.

In a world of confusion Jesus clearly states that there are reliable principles upon which our lives can be built. Whenever we are tempted, it is most likely we are being faced with either complete falsehood, or more likely with half-truths that present themselves in guise as light. When we know the truth, these temptations are seen in a different light and immediately begin to lose their power. Jesus said, "If you hold to my teaching, you are really my disciples, then you will know the truth, and the truth will set you free." John 8:31-32.

We live in a world where the family has disintegrated to the point where in many communities there are few children being raised by both parents. Where money is either not managed at all or managed with value systems that are out of balance with love, justice, and life purpose that has lasting meaning. In our world today, unresolved conflict routinely results in violence. In this kind of world, Jesus wants us to dwell in Him, so we can be a light on the hill giving hope, showing that there is direction, and a way to live in the midst of this confusion. This is good news indeed.

Dwelling in Christ means holding to his clear teachings, and allowing Him to live them out through you, in your life, in this world, day to day.

8. It is a relationship in which in spite of our weakness and insignificance on our own, we are given the privilege of partnership with him in the greatest mission ever undertaken.

Jesus taught us to pray **"your kingdom come, your will be done on earth as it is in heaven"**. God wants to use us for kingdom purposes. We have no strength of our own; we derive all of our strength from Him. We derive our very life from him, yet even as every branch in a well pruned grape vine bears grapes so does every branch that remains in Christ bear fruit.

We tend to despise weakness, yet God never despises weakness.

> "Blessed are the poor in spirit, for theirs is the kingdom of heaven.
>
> Blessed are they that mourn for they will be comforted.
>
> Blessed are the meek for they will inherit the earth." Matt. 5:3-5
>
> "God opposes the proud but gives grace to the humble." I Peter 5:5

"My Grace is sufficient for you, for my power is made perfect in weakness". II Cor. 12:9

<u>God wants to use us first of all, right where we are</u>. He wants to do this even with the brand new believer who truly trusts in Christ, and who reflects that trust. He wants as he lives through us to begin to influence those around them even as Eric in the previous incident. We must first be found faithful in little things, if we are to be entrusted with larger things. Eric did not try to witness, the life changing power of Christ, made such a difference in him, that it attracted attention. It called attention to the power and glory of God, such that faith in and obedience to God became an option.

As we progress in our Christian faith; <u>those that God places around us will always be an area of responsibility</u>. It may not continue to be the area of primary ministry activity depending on where God places us, as for example in an area of specialized ministry, but it should always be an area, in which as we dwell in Christ we are listening for his instruction.

We need to have an awareness of the larger scope of God's mission. Again, note His prayer; God wants his kingdom to come, here on this earth. It is not enough to save someone for heaven. God wants to be both present in, and Lord of, the world in which we live. How does he want to use us in that process?

Are we listening? If so God will guide us step by step.

More on God's total mission will be discussed in The Christ Follower's Interaction with Unbelievers

9. It is a relationship in which Christ gives sustaining power. It is neither possible nor necessary for us to muster up the strength. He gives both the power to work and to choose. We must provide the willingness to draw on Him for his power.

Christians often fall into two groups, those who give in to the philosophy that we sin in word, thought, and deed every day, so let's not worry too much about it. Or the group that consciously or subconsciously believes that it is up to them, and become trapped in another "works" effort, that then often results in hypocrisy, or despair.

Neither of these situations is necessary, nor results from good theology. God lavishes his love upon us, and graciously gives everything we need for a life of godliness. Yes, God indeed gives us the grace of forgiveness, He urges us to come. We must continually come because, in this life sins of ignorance, and weakness will always be near. John tells us, "If we claim to be without sin, we deceive ourselves and the truth is not in us. If we confess our sins, he is faithful and just and will forgive us our sins and purify us from all unrighteousness. -------My dear children I write this to you so that you will not sin, but if anyone does sin, we have one who speaks to the Father in our defense—Jesus Christ the Righteous One. He is the atoning sacrifice for our sins,—"I John 1:8 -2:2

This same John in this same book goes on to tell us that "He" (Jesus) appeared to take away sins of lawlessness. (See I John 3:4-6) Having defined sin as lawlessness, John goes on to say, "No one who is born of God will continue to sin, because God's seed remains in him; he cannot go on sinning because he has been born of God. This is how we know who the children of God are and who the children of the devil are: Anyone who does not do what is right is not a child of God; nor is anyone who does not love is brother." I John 3:9-10

. John is here speaking of sins of rebellion, willful deliberate persistent sin. It is evidence of unbelief, not just doubt and weakness. Repentance occurs when a person realizes and admits that they are wrong, and chose to stop going away from God, turns around and begins to go with God. One cannot at the same time persist in active rebellion against someone, who they trust deeply and whom they love deeply.

When we come to dwell in Christ, by faith surrendering ourselves to His love and mercy; when we accept the truth of his word about Him, ourselves, and the world around us, His power will free us from sins of rebellion. God's power breaks the power of sin as rebellion. We cannot do this but God can, and will if we are willing.

As we then dwell in Christ, we need not worry about being able to dwell or remain in Him. He will do it in us, if we will let Him. It is His power that enables faith; it is His power that enables our choices; it is ours to choose.

10. It is a relationship in which all the resources necessary to accomplish what he wants to do through us are fully at our disposal as we ask and receive from Him.

"And I will do whatever you ask in my name, so that the son may bring glory to the Father. You may ask me for anything in my name and I will do it. If you love me, you will obey what I command. John 14:13-15.

"If you remain in me, and my words remain in you, ask whatever you wish, and it will be given you." John 15:7.

While God wants to and will supply our personal needs that are in accordance to his will; I do not believe that is the intended thrust of what Jesus is saying to His disciples in this missional section of scripture. **I believe these promises are specifically missional statements. They are intended to clearly show us that as we dwell in Him, as we are about**

His business, when we are acting in obedience to His command; we will not lack anything we need to complete our mission. If we ask in His Name we will receive.

When Peter and John came to the temple gate called beautiful, and came across the man crippled from birth described in Acts 3, they were drawing on these resource that Jesus described when they spoke to the crippled man and in the name of Jesus, commanded that he walk, followed by an extended hand to help him up.

George Mueller Christian evangelist and Director of Ashley Down Orphanage in 1800"s Bristol, England cared for 10,024 orphans during his lifetime. He deliberately and purposefully never announced the needs required to do this or requested funds from others. Instead he asked in prayer. His reason for doing this: he wanted God to be glorified, and he wanted others to know that God could be trusted to do what He says he will do.

When we are fully engaged in doing what God entrusts us with as individuals who are dwelling in him we will never lack the resources to do His will. Failure may often accompany our efforts, due to our attempts to walk in our own strength, our lack of faith, or our downright disobedience, but the resources we need to do what he wants is always available.

Discussion Questions?

What does it mean to you personally to dwell or abide in Christ?

For you personally, what struggles are most a part of this relationship? Boredom? Rebellion? Impatience? Indifference? Silence? Guilt? Presumption?

What is the connection between Dwelling in Christ and interaction with unbelievers?

B. Listening to God

As a child Samuel heard God's voice 3 times before having been prompted by Eli, he recognized the voice as that of God and listened to his instructions. Thereafter throughout his life God continued to speak to Samuel. God's messages to Samuel ranged from God's rebuke to both Eli himself, and to King David; they ranged from messages for other people, to instructions for battle. God's manner of speaking to Samuel was unique, He will however, speak to anyone who will listen.

Hebrews 1:1 tells us, "In the past God spoke to our forefathers through the prophets at many times and in various ways, but in these last days he has spoken to us by his Son."

Our generation with voices from around the world and information overload is often a very confusing place. In this confusion, how does God speak to us? Based on the history of God's unique ways as he has dealt with many individuals and circumstances, I believe it will be unique to each of us, but there will always be certain patterns that will hold true.

First, God's message will never be contrary to his nature as God; his Love, His Holiness, His Justice. Second, God's message will never be contrary to what He has already revealed in His written word. Third, there will always be a direct correlation between Jesus as the Word of God, and the written word. Thus any message to us will directly correspond. Many actions can be taken with little thought, when we seem to be nudged by God's Spirit, if they are in line with right and good. However the greater the consequence may be of an action, the more we need to check our motives, our source of wisdom, and be sure of the source of our inner "light".

In light of confusion of voices, whenever we think we have a word from God, we need to immediately, and <u>always check it against his word</u>. Whatever word we may believe we have, it has come to us as a part of our self-talk and thinking process. That self-talk is the result of every experience we have ever had, every vicarious experience you have had by watching someone else, in person, through a book or movie. It can be influenced by our own conscious and subconscious desires, good and bad. It can be influenced by direct and indirect activity of evil spirits. And yes, thankfully, it can be the direct or indirect influence of the Spirit of God. The scriptures themselves teach us to try the spirits to see if they are from God.

Someone noted the following pitfalls of Solomon:

1. Solomon trusted his mind more than the Lord.
2. Solomon trusted his experience more than the Lord.
3. Solomon trusted his eyes more than the Lord.
4. Solomon trusted his heart more than the Lord. The Scripture includes many evidences of Solomon's wisdom; it also describes much of his folly. If Solomon who is noted for his wisdom had these pitfalls, we need to take heed. Protect your mind. Fill it with the **Word.**

Battle for the Mind

Our minds are battlefields. You may not be what you think you are, but you are what you think! He is a fool who thinks he can keep on thinking what he has always thought and get a different result. Our decisions, and consequently our attitudes and behavior, are always based on our thought process. These thought processes are based on our circumstance and our reaction to them, what we place or allow to be placed into our minds. We then filter this through our own internal filter system. This filter system is largely subconscious. In other words it is so much a part of us that we do not even think of it and are not normally even aware of it.

This internal system consists of five primary things. Our core beliefs, or unconscious rules; our life values; our own point of reference; our self-talk, or the questions that we habitually ask ourselves; and the emotional state that we experience moment to moment.

This thinking process has radical implications for our future, our relationship with God, our ability to listen, and our willingness to obey what God tells us to do.

Unthinking Christians often avoid insights gained in the scientific community, especially those relating to our psychic nature. Yet in this area as in any area of study, as in any Science, it must start with what God has created. When individuals discover truth; it is still truth whether they believe in God or not.

Studies have shown that when behavior patterns are entrenched as they become in all of our lives, these patterns can only be changed through a crisis event in our lives or through constant repletion.

Scriptures show God working and attempting to move us toward himself and into deep relationship with himself through both Crisis and constant repetition.

In Romans 7-8 the Apostle Paul makes reference to two different mind sets:

There is the mind that is <u>set on self</u>, and there is the mind that is <u>set on Christ</u>.

In other words there is a subconscious core of beliefs, life values, points of reference, habitual questions, and emotional responses that the scriptures identify as the sinful mind or the mind set on self. As long this sinful mind remains in place, our decisions about what to focus on, what things mean to us, and what we will do to create the results that we want will continue to be independent of God, self-centered and dominated by the flesh, the world and the devil.

Being separated from God, man learns to seek meaning and purpose in life through what he can experience through his physical fleshly existence. Life centers on self, and he becomes his own little god. His life is characterized by pride, self-exaltation and independence from the God who made him. These characteristics may be seen clearly in some in the raw totally selfish unconcern for others. It may be seen in others as well disguised selfishness, high morality, and high achievements.

Persons who have not come to Faith in Jesus Christ often pursue self-centered lifestyles without thought, conflict, insight, or remorse. However, once a person has trusted Christ, is forgiven and begins to have the light of God's Spirit shining in their life, they often enter a time of major inner conflict much as Paul describes in Romans 7. "For what I do is not the good I want to do; no, the evil I do not want to do—this I keep on doing. Rom. 7:19. These persons find that they have a divided self. On the one hand with the conscious mind they want what God wants. On the other with the unconscious or subconscious mind they do not want to obey God.

The battle is fought within your mind. Hence a shift in mind set is required. For some this may be hard fought, for others perhaps subtle, yet nevertheless a very decisive shift is essential. You must move from a mind set on self, to a mind that is set on Christ; from a mind that is self-centered to a mind that is Christ centered.

Christ put it this way in Mathew 16:24-27. We must be willing to lose our life to save it.

Speaking psychologically to achieve a shift of thinking on the subconscious level there must be either constant repetition, or a crisis situation.

Speaking Biblically I believe there must first be a crisis situation, followed by constant repetition. **I believe Christ is first calling us to a Crisis; we must die to self.** A shift here is a radical reinterpretation to the subconscious of what we will focus on, what things mean, and what we will do to achieve what we want. But it is more than that. When we really come to the place where we are willing to die to self and surrender fully to the Lordship of Christ, it is not something we have achieved on our own, but something his Spirit is enabling. He meets us at that crisis point with cleansing of our inner self, with the fullness of Himself. He enables the change. The first disciples came to the place of surrender as they prayerfully obeyed Christ's instructions to wait at Jerusalem. Their lives were changed when the Holy Spirit filled and purified them at Pentecost.

But what about the day to day issues of life? Does a moment of crisis suddenly transport me to an instant and constant victory over sin and self-defeating behaviors and attitudes? Absolutely not, as the apostle Paul said, I die daily. I will say from personal experience, once a person confronts the issue, and completely surrenders to Christ, it will probably never be as difficult another time. Once we really see that God's will for our life is really not only good but best, that he has a perfect plan, that while it may include hardship and difficulty, it is worth it, even unto death; then we are able to come to that point of faith, and surrender of the will that allows God to do his work in our lives. Often it is not until we see the futility of our own efforts to change and the mess of directing our own lives that we are willing to take that step of faith, but that is not always so, if we have been taking the baby steps one at a time He often leads us into it without much of a struggle. The day to day issues are dealt with and we are transformed by the renewing of the mind, as daily we remind ourselves of truth by immersion in the word of God, high quality books, clear biblical preaching, and association with persons who also seek to abide in Christ.

The battle for the mind is particularly important in the issue of listening to God, because God generally will not guide people who are not willing to obey. Adam and Eve first disobey God because of a battle for the mind. They were deceived by Satan's subtle twist of the truth, such that they believed Satan, and disbelieved God. Jesus himself was tempted in the wilderness as Satan again attempted to twist the truth. Jesus resisted temptation by presenting the truth. As this battle is waged in our minds, the battle is with truth issues. We can never over power Satan in his attempts to destroy us, we must out truth him, even as Jesus overcame Satan with the truth. **Truth in the hands of the Spirit of God is the liberating agent**, hence the importance again, not only of a thorough knowledge of the word of God, but of our constant daily immersion in it. I cannot over emphasize this. Our search of the Scriptures is essentially a search for truth; the truth about the world we live in, the truth about ourselves, the truth about God and who he really is. The more that we understand the truth, the easier it will be to avoid deception and call on the Lord with strong faith in our times of need. The Word of God in the hands of the Spirit of God is power in our lives. When we really, and consistently get into it, walk in it, obey it, God in His Spirit will find a way to guide us through it. He will not only use it to change our lives from the inside out, but will impact the lives of those he has placed around us.

In contest with the prophets of Baal, after their failure, Elijah had called down fire from heaven, which had consumed the water drenched sacrifices, showing God to be God. Yet following this when His life was threatened by Jezebel, Elijah ran for his life. As he reflects on His situation, he begins to feel sorry for himself. He asked God to take his life, feeling that he is all alone, and a failure. Interestingly God does not speak to him through powerful wind, fire, or an earthquake, rather through a still small voice. God reminded him of the truth, the whole truth. He had not failed, he was not alone, and there were 7000 others who had not bowed their knees to Baal. James 5:17 tells us that "Elijah was a man just like us." After the emotional stress of his encounter with the prophets of Baal, he was physically and emotionally drained. He experienced the normal symptoms common to man. He needed food, rest, and a clear perspective to recover. He was able to hear the still small voice, because of constant practice. He heard in the crisis hour because he had practiced listening to God. Because He listened God was able to correct the distortion of truth, with the full truth.

When we speak of listening to God we are also talking about knowing and doing the will of God on a moment to moment, day to day basis. If we are, in fact, dwelling in Christ, and He in us, then that is what we desire in our lives. The question is, is this what we really want? Really, really want; want it bad enough to learn how to listen? Listening on this level involves listening with the ears of the heart, with a heart for what God really wants in me and around me.

Much of our behavior, even when we are attempting to listen and respond to God's voice, will still be imperfect. We are learners. We still have human ignorance and weakness. God honors our faith in him, our willingness to obey, not the perfection or imperfection of our action.

Remember Peter and his vision? We also often have preconceived notions, and God has to beat us over the head to get our attention, so that we can hear what he has to say.

From Pentecost on, those who dwell in Christ have had the Holy Spirit as their infallible guide to truth. He will work through the written word of God, and his indwelling presence to guide us, if our ears are really open to hear.

We need to focus on the relationship that Christ has invited us into, to grasp fully the opportunity, and means of hearing God's voice available since Pentecost. In John 14-17 the interaction of the triune God is clearly described. The three are one.

Believers are invited into this relationship. True we are invited in as a branch on a vine. We are not the vine, yet we are to be "In Christ", and Christ is to be in us. Instead of God coming to us from outside to speak to us, He is to be in us to speak to us through His Spirit. When he is dwelling within, he does not need an audible voice. He has an inner voice.

There is one other indispensable facet of this listening relationship, which must not be ignored or underestimated. <u>God has already spoken and revealed Himself</u> <u>through the Word</u>. "All Scripture is God- breathed and is useful for teaching, rebuking, correcting, and training in righteousness so that the man of God may be thoroughly equipped for every good work." II Tim. 3:16-17

God is certainly capable of speaking to us, aside from what he has already spoken. However, it is not only presumptuous to expect him to do so, it not likely that we would hear and understand without the training of His word. If we are not studiously equipping ourselves with knowledge of what he already is saying through the word, we open ourselves to seriously being deceived by Satan.

When we couple a growing understanding of his word with the presence of the Holy Spirit in our lives we can expect God to speak. Prayer can become a two way conversation, as we read the word, meditate, consider first what it actually says, and prayerfully consider what God may say to us through it.

We do not have to be a *Bible* expert, to have God speak through His word. The newest babe in Christ can begin to hear from God, if they will seek Him. We do have to be listening, have to be willing to obey. God will not show himself to those who are unwilling to follow.

If we are not hearing from God, we need to check specifically to see if there is sin in our lives. Am I involved with any wrong relationships which are not pleasing to God? Am I adding to the confusing voices by adding poisonous thoughts through what I am reading, viewing, and listening to outside of His word? It is great to have freedom in Christ. However we are never free to ignore the Spirits check without again becoming a slave to sin. Are there circumstances that I am facing where God has already, been speaking, I know what he wants and I am ignoring Him? Is there good that I already know to do that I have not done?

Much of what God has to say to us when we begin to listen will be for our own relationship with Him, and with those immediately around us. It will have to do with our attitude, and behavior. As we respond to his voice in these areas, he will begin to lead us out and beyond.

A young man recently asked me how he could know what God's will was for his life. What he really wanted to know was: what career path should I follow? Who should I marry? But God does not start there; he starts with the little things. He rarely gives us a blue print for where he wants to take us. He takes us one step, one day at a time. He says; come follow me. He is more interested in the relationship. If He gave us all the details, we would not need to walk with Him.

Much of God's guidance comes as we are in the middle of a situation. Ideally we have started the day deliberately and consciously with God. Perhaps we are at work, conflict starts, I pray even as I react. Wisdom stored in memory from the word, is brought to my mind by the Spirit, and I respond accordingly. Whether conflict is resolved or not, God may use my attitude to his glory. Remember, people can never be attracted to a god who is nothing in their eyes. But when God is glorified and lifted up, he can draw people to Himself.

Suppose I arrive at an unbelieving friend's house, and he informs me he is leaving his wife, or that his wife is leaving him. Suppose any number of other situations. God can and will give guidance as we seek him. That guidance may not be to say or do anything except to be a good listener. There are plenty of situations in which we need to prayerfully seek guidance over a period of time. However, I find many, many more in which, I see opportunity before me, a thought comes to get involved, there is nothing wrong, with doing so, possibly good could come. So I act upon my thought, assuming it has come from God.

We have recently moved to a totally new community. We are seeking to get acquainted in the community with other Christians, as well as to make friends with unbelievers around us. There was a vacant house next property over in this semi-rural community. Watching from the distance I was not sure if people were moving in or out, but this day I saw a U-Haul that was definitely coming in. I thought this would be a good opportunity to meet them and perhaps be of some help. So I walked over. I met an elderly couple, at least as old as I. I asked if I could be of help. They looked at me with a very overwhelmed look that I cannot quite describe. She was limping badly from a failed knee surgery. He had a bad heart. I said, I think I may be able get another old man to help us. So I called a neighbor, whom I had recently met at the Church. He left dinner uneaten and came and helped. We unloaded the truck and made two new friends. Was God in it? I believe so.

Mary Geegh, missionary to India, in her little pamphlet, God Guides, tells of seeking guidance related to a feeling of friction between herself and a colleague with 10 children who didn't seem to be carrying her load. One morning the thought came to her, "take her a fresh egg". This seemed ridiculous, (a dozen might be reasonable, but one?) so she ignored it until at noon she came home to her wide open house and discovered a chicken in her armchair that got up to reveal a fresh egg. After further argument with God she delivered the egg, sending it in with a young son to the mother. Latter in the evening the mother inquired how she happened to bring the egg. Mary reveled that it was God's guidance. The mother revealed that she had not had enough that morning for everyone, and had gone without. The egg was just what she needed. This was just the beginning as God used this incident to teach listening to him, which lead to a whole chain of changed lives, all starting because one person listened, obeyed and provided one egg.

It is the accumulation of thousands of little day to day actions where we have listened to God that results in him touching lives and seeing individuals come to faith. It is the accumulation of actions of Christ followers all across a city, or rural community that can totally change the community. It is the accumulation of actions from millions of Christ followers, each really allowing Christ to live in and through them that can literally change the world where live. **We are the body of Christ; he wants to work through us right where we are.**

Discussion questions:

What is meant by listening to God?

How do I know if God is speaking to me?

Does God always speak in the same way? Does He speak to some people differently than others?

If I am uncertain what should I do?

What is the difference between listening as we read, study, and pray with God's word at the center, and other forms of meditation?

When we are reading the Word, praying, etc., will we always hear God accurately? Why? Why not?

What might the result have looked like if Jim Baker (or any other minister, or lay person) had really been actively listening to God?

What will the results look like if you really listen?

C. Obedience: doing what the head of the body instructs

There is no real obedience without faith and love; aside from these the spirit of obedience is lost. Dwelling in Christ involves all three. Much Christian preaching and literature seems to forget the intimate relationship of faith and behavior. <u>We always, to the extent of our ability, behave based on what we **actually** believe.</u> Faith and action are as inseparable, as in any cause and effect situation. I hit a ball (cause), something will happen (effect); whether a broken window, or a home run.

Our bodies are designed to operate efficiently as a united whole, as every part receives and follows the instructions of the head (technically the brain). When some portion does not respond to instructions from the head, we know that we are not healthy, whether the failure results from emotional issues, fatigue, or other perhaps catastrophic break down.

The body of Christ, of which we are only one member, operates in a similar manner. Christ is always the Head. Our relationship with him is unique in that we have a choice. We can choose to obey, or disobey. When one member of the body fails to obey, the body does not function as it should, and Christ's mission through His body is compromised. It may not seem that significant for one member to fail, but when it is multiplied across the Church the effects are devastating. Moreover, when **you** fail to obey, it is those in **your circle** of influence that are most directly affected, whether that be family member, friend, co-worker, or neighbor.

Obedience is the test of your whole relationship. It defines whether anything else in your whole relationship is valid. It matters not that you really get with it in worship service. It is irrelevant that you get blessed by the preacher's messages. It makes no difference if you volunteer with the hospice, or just got home from a mission trip. If you will not do what Jesus Christ tells you to do, there is something wrong in your relationship with him that needs to be corrected, **now.**

Failure to obey is common, and stems from several root causes. For convenience in looking at them, let's divide them in two general areas: first those resulting from willful disobedience; second those resulting from weakness and ignorance.

Willful disobedience stems from lack of faith, and/or lack of love. If it stems from a stubborn resistant heart of refusal to believe in spite of clear knowledge of Jesus Christ, you are in serious spiritual jeopardy, and need to confess your sin, repent and ask God for a new heart. If it stems from persistent doubt, weak faith, shallow love, **you need to start with getting better acquainted with Jesus Christ**. The more that you know Him; the more that you will love and trust Him.

There are several ways to approach this. First, is in your own time alone with him and the Word. If it is not already part of your life, let me remind you. You cannot get along without it. You cannot get acquainted with Jesus Christ or anyone else for that matter without spending time with them. You must get into his word in serious study. This is not a matter of obligation. It is an issue of life. As you get into God's word, you need to begin to talk with him. Share everything with him.

Seek to understand Him and His ways. A good place to start is the Gospel of John. Particularly pay attention every time He says: "I am".

Second, get involved with a small group of other believer's, even if you have to form a group yourself. You do not have to be an expert, just someone who wants along with others to know and experience Jesus Christ in your life. Read and pray together, with a commitment to keep each other's confidences. Learn from each other's successes and failures. Encourage each other. Learn to be accountable to others who love you and are themselves committed to wholeheartedly following Jesus Christ. I consider this type of small group equal to, if not more important than Sunday worship.

Third, attempt to be part of a church where the word is preached with clarity and where obedience to God, not simply the rules imposed by man is encouraged. I do not encourage church hopping. Even tough situations may be used of God, however, if your church situation is keeping you from obeying God you need to change.

Fourth, begin to read high quality Christian books. Especially read books that will assist you in the hard questions of faith that you wrestle with. Read books that help you really see who Jesus is in his full manhood, and full Godhood.

If your disobedience stems from ignorance and weakness, a lot of the remedy is the same. Ignorance of what I should do and don't do is still sin, it needs the forgiveness of God. Ignorance of what I should do wherein I remain ignorant because I am lazy and refuse to "study to show yourself approved, a workman who does not need to be ashamed" (my of paraphrase II Tim. 2:15), borders on willful sin. We will never in this life be free from sins of ignorance and weakness, but as we walk with Christ, grow in our relationship with Him, His Grace is sufficient to assist us in these areas. As God makes me aware of an area of ignorance, I need not remain ignorant. As God makes me aware of areas of weakness, I can seek His strength. I can seek the assistance of Christian brothers or sisters, who can encourage and help me. God's strength is made perfect in my weakness as I yield it to Him. "

Crucial issues are involved as we face the realities of living in the "flesh" (sinful nature) or living in the "Spirit".* Most disobedience stems from still living in the flesh. The Apostle Paul describes this battle in Romans 7-8. (See previous discussion P.) There is much controversy over just how these passages are to be interpreted. It does seem to be absolutely clear however, that we cannot win the battle on our own. It requires the strength of God's Spirit. When we fully surrender our very selves to God, (die to self), God's spirit lives within us to accomplish what we cannot do in our strength. It is only in living, in the strength of the Spirit, that I am enabled to obey God.

*(The Greek uses two distinct term, soma or body, and sarx or flesh. These should not be confused. The body is not evil. Yet the sinful

nature (sarx) inhabits us, and sometimes in our spiritual battles may feel indistinguishable from our bodies.)

This subject is approached from different angles, by devout Christians of various theological backgrounds. My background and training is in the Wesleyan Armenian tradition, however I have worshiped and served together with those of other traditions for long periods of time. Each lends perspective and balance to the others. "Now we see but a poor reflection in a mirror; then we shall see face to face. --- And now these three remain: faith, hope, and love. But the greatest of these is love. I Cor. 13:12-13.

Wesleyans would see a person made alive by the Spirit with initial, or the start of sanctification received at conversion, as the Holy Spirit first enters our life. This may be followed by a long or short period, as well as relapses to the struggle described in Romans 7:7-25. This may be succeeded by death to self, full surrender of oneself to God, resulting in entire sanctification, or heart purity. This is seen not at all as perfection of life, rather as purity of conscious motive toward God and man. John Wesley states in His writings that he doubted that 1 in 30 who arrived at this point maintained it. Yet it is in this surrender that God is able to use us.

Other large portions of the Church down play many of these distinctions, and instead emphasis the acceptance of Jesus Christ as the Lord of our lives, not just our savior.

Regardless of the theological persuasion, I believe that each of us who are serious followers of Jesus Christ, at some point following conversion, become aware of a proneness to sin, and recognize a need to die to self, and surrender to God. If we do this, he not only enables us to dwell in him, to really hear Him speaking, but also to live in obedience to Him. It is only in this relationship of dwelling, listening and obeying that God can really begin to fully use our lives for His purposes. It is only in this relationship that we can get ourselves out of the way and He can use us to bring others to Himself.

Discussion questions:

What is the connection between faith, love, and obedience?

If there is obedience without faith, or love, what would it mean?

If a person claims to have faith in or love for God, but does not obey, what are the implications?

What first step do you need to take to be fully obedient to God at this moment?

What steps do you need to take to continue in obedience?

What is implied for you time in the Word? Do you need someone else to help you be accountable?

What is implied in your family relationships, in your work relationships, your church relationships?

What is implied in your use of your time, your abilities, and your treasure?

If God is really stretching you right now what do you need in graciousness from others and especially in accepting God's grace in your life right now?

D. Giving and receiving Grace

Observation of both the Scripture and life clearly demonstrate that there are serious consequences when we fail to obey God. These consequences are not only to us, but also to those persons who might have benefited from our obedience.

Our understanding of these consequences may differ depending on our basic theological understandings. Some would attempt to avoid all of these differences of opinion by never discussing them, or perhaps never even studying them. I prefer to do both, because I both want to know God as much as possible, and because I believe that knowledge of their distinctions help each of us to understand ourselves and to more fully live out our lives "in Christ". Regardless of years of study each of us perceive only partially. The more I know the more I realize how much I do not know.

Here are some of my observations.

God has created this world with order. There are laws that govern it. These are an inescapable part of this universe. If I jump off a cliff without cooperating with some other of God's laws that defy gravity, there will be natural consequence when I hit the bottom.

God also created the spiritual universe. There are laws that govern it. They are just as inescapable as in the physical universe. It is not that God so much imposes a law upon us, as that again they are built into the very nature of the universe, into the very nature of man and his relationship with the spiritual universe. God has made these laws clear, starting with the Ten Commandments, along with his promises and warnings to Israel.

These laws have not changed.

However, with Christ, something new has been introduced. "a righteousness from God, apart from law has been made known, ----This righteousness from God comes through faith in Jesus Christ to all who believe." Rom. 3:21-22

Yes something new has been introduced; it is something none of us deserve; **it is called Grace**. We have all jumped off the cliff and God has intervened with another law completely, the law of His Grace which can salvage our fall.

This law of Grace does not just operate at the moment of my conversion. It operates continually. It operates in the lives of unbeliever, giving them opportunity to be saved. It operated fully in the lives of believers as they continue to dwell in Him. Our absolute need of this grace is clearly seen if we are at all self-conscious, and look at our attitudes and actions. We desperately need his gracious power in our lives to live right, and we desperately need his gracious forgiveness for where we do not.

But there is yet another whole arena of grace. <u>It is that arena in which we give or fail to give grace to others around us.</u> It is that arena in which we make it possible for others around us to receive grace.

In the United States, conservative Christians are not known for their graciousness. They are known for their condemnation of the sins of others around them. I have to seriously question the extent to which we can receive grace, if we refuse grace to those with whom we have contact. To love is to offer grace, yet especially in the conservative Christian world we are far more known for our call for judgement than we are for our graciousness. If we are so busy or preoccupied with even our other Christian work that we fail to be gracious and offer grace to those who surround us, <u>how can we with good conscience expect it in our own life</u>? If we set ourselves up as the world's judge and jury, how dare we then demand God's grace in our lives'? I say demand deliberately, because many are so much into a "grace" culture, that God could not possible demand 'right behavior". We cannot gain salvation by works, so of course I will receive his grace.

Failure to be gracious is not just a problem for you. It is a problem for me. If I walk into the store, to pay for my gas, and there is a person ahead who is buying lotto tickets, scratching them off, buying another, etc. while I wait, intruding on my over busy schedule; am I gracious? When I see some of the obvious consequences of a sinful lifestyle; am I critical, or am I compassionate? In other words am I gracious, giving to others goodness they do not deserve?

Graciousness to others costs me nothing except the prerogative to play god, yet the benefits could be eternal. I do not deserve God's grace to me. Much of my struggles are because of my own ignorant or weak decisions, yet God still gives his grace to me.

Jesus conditioned God's forgiveness of us, on our forgiveness of those who have caused us loss. We can admit freely the injustice of the man in Jesus story who was forgiven a debt of millions who then refused to forgive a few dollars. Yet, we can struggle majorly when we have received one of this life's seemingly major or even minor wounds. Tragically when we fail to give grace we not only cut ourselves off from grace, but we often also cut the unbeliever off from grace as we give those around us an inaccurate picture of Christ Himself, who we profess lives in us.

Dwelling in Christ involves both giving and receiving grace. Fortunately, the more we really acknowledge and freely receive God's grace, the more easily we can give it to others. The more that we see them through God's eye's the easier it is to give grace to them. The more we give grace, the easier it is to do it again.

Receiving and giving grace is an in depth part of dwelling in Christ and He is us.

Discussion questions?

Would your neighbors consider your Church gracious? Would your family and friends consider you gracious?

If not what do you think this does to your credibility and to Christ's attractiveness?

What can be done to make you gracious? in your time alone with God? in your daily activities?

Are you in need of opening yourself fully to the grace of God in order that it may more fully flow through you to others?

Section Three

The Christ follower's
interaction with unbelievers

Letting Christ live His life in and through you

God is a spirit. You a believer cannot see him, certainly your unbelieving neighbor cannot. Except for the body of Christ, **God has no visible presence** in this world. Evidences of His existence, evidences of His presence are here, however, they can be easily missed, misinterpreted, and dismissed by the unbeliever; remember they are yet dead in their sin. As such they are blind to spiritual truth. As such it is unfair to expect them to know and understand as we do. Even Jesus himself spoke in parables for this reason.

In light of this, it is certainly unfair to attempt to hold unbelievers to Christian standards of morality. Only through Christ we should attain Christian standards of morality. Yet often not only do professed Christians fail to attain, they just as often, are quick to judge others who place no value on such morality, and see no valid reason why they should.

Here at the very beginning as we try to understand how to relate effectively to unbelievers, we need to try to view things from their shoes.

Consider the world that we live in and its history of just the last 100 years. It is a world in which wars that have killed multiplied million, have been an ongoing way of life. It is a world in which terrorism is a threat with few obvious ways to protect one's self or fight back. It is a world in which repeatedly additional millions have been put to death in ethnic cleansing, purges of unwanted peoples. It is a world in which starvation of millions has been an ongoing way of life in spite of the fact that in this same world there is capability of raising enough food. It is a world in which the difference between the haves and the have not's has been sharp in contrast, made much worse because the differences are exaggerated even more by the apparent beauty and affluence declared by media. It is a world in which the media regularly spotlights a famous, often religious person, for their immorality. It is a world in which the haves, exploit the have not's to maintain their edge. And now with modern technology, the rich and powerful, many times do it remotely and maintain their safety. It is a world in which even among the haves, people are not happy. Divorce is rampant, and it is becoming a rarity if children are raised by both their own parents.

I ask you,

If this were you, living the life described above, if your own experience was the only source, without other sources of knowing, would you believe in a God that exists, especially that he is a God of love? Would you believe that this God was one that you could trust with your life?

If you were one of these individuals, if you had no personal knowledge through a real living person that demonstrated God's love, could you believe that He does love you? Without someone who showed you that God has a personal interest in you individually, without someone who enabled you to see that while God does allow suffering that he allows it because it is the result of mankind's own choices. Without personal knowledge through someone you trust, could you come to trust this God? Could you believe in God without first being enabled to see how God in his love, has and is providing a way back and a way through? Could you, would you, without any of this come to faith in Jesus Christ?

Relatively few would. Someone might read the Word, or other Christian literature, get saved and successfully find a live healthy church, but it is rare. Even if they get saved, getting into a good church is difficult. I know. I travel. I have moved. I have tried to get people in. Most are closed societies, or worse yet orthodox, but stone cold and unhelpful to struggling Christians let alone unbelievers. You can always attend, but often cannot get in. There is a major difference!

People do not come to Christ in a vacuum. In order to come to Christ there must first in a general sense be an awareness that God in fact exists, there must be an awareness that God has some tangible answer to life's difficulties. There must be some prior knowledge that; Jesus in fact is God, not just a god, not one among many, but The God. There must be a felt need, a reason for coming.

In order for these things to become true. **There must be someone to show that it is possible, someone to show the way.**

This is where you and I as part of the body of Christ play our part. As we live in Christ and He lives in us, He begins to make Himself known.

We pursue in the materials that immediately follow what it means in practice to show the way. Some of what is said, reviews and reemphasizes earlier material.

Understanding and being involved with the Ministry of reconciliation

What **"in the world"** are we to do?

Rather than producing some perfect automats to show us who God is, who a perfect holy God is; God has chosen to take a weak, broken, imperfect people who through faith are in the process of being transformed; to communicate himself through them to other broken, dead-to-God, people who do not yet have faith.

When contact is made person to person by people of faith who are known, then people with walls—walls of fear, walls of pride, walls of prejudice; introverts, and extroverts began to see, begin to listen, often when it doesn't seem possible, or that they are listening.

We are now attempting to **focus and apply** many of the principles earlier discussed. These principles apply to **"the Believers interaction with unbelievers"**, in the World in which we live.

One pastor laughed when viewing these materials, and first seeing this phrase, "in the world". However, use of the phrase "in the world" is deliberate.

So often the church attempts to escape, to avoid the world. Many church people perceive themselves, "believers" as only strangers in this world, aliens, persecuted, not of this world. Thus this world is not their home, they are only traveling through. They must make every effort to protect themselves, and thus do not want to get their hands dirty. Yet, while this may represent a partial grasp of truth, this was not Jesus attitude.

Jesus deliberately came to this world. He "made himself nothing, taking the very nature of a servant, being made in human likeness. And being found in appearance as a man he humbles himself and became obedient to death—even death of the cross!"

For Jesus, God who became a man (the Word become flesh), this was a little like a man becoming an ant in order to help an ant understand what a man was, to so identify himself with the ants, that he did not just become the queen ant, but one of the worker ants.

Rather than withdraw from the world, Jesus deliberately came to this world and as a man immersed Himself in our world.

Jesus's interaction with people was such that Luke records, "Now the tax collectors and "sinners" were all gathering around to hear him. But the Pharisees and teachers of the law muttered, "This man welcomes sinners and eats with them." Jesus response was to tell the parable of the lost sheep, the lost coin, and the lost son.

To focus clearly on <u>what we are to do "in this world"</u> we must keep in focus <u>what Jesus came to do "in this world"</u>.

Aside from the atonement, **Jesus primary purpose in coming to the world was to make the nature of God known to the world through His personal presence.** <u>He did this as a **servant**</u>. Jesus Glorified the Father, that the father's glory might be seen, that the world would believe. **I.E. the world would only believe when they begin to see correctly, who God is.**

"The Word became flesh and made His dwelling among us. We have seen his glory, the glory of the one and only, who came from the Father, full of grace and truth. --- No one has ever seen God, but God the one and only, who is at the Father's side, has made Him known." John 1:14, 18.

Jesus came to make His father known through his personal presence. **Now he wants to make his personal presence known by being in-fleshed in us.**

Albert and his wife were neighbors in their mid-eighties. They were life-time members of another denomination. He had been active in church, and served on the board etc.

Albert was very picky about his neighbors. He didn't like noise, disruptions or most neighbors. However, our seven year old daughter, with her big brown eyes did not know this when she engaged him in conversation over the back fence. I ignored his often negative attitudes. I often practically insisted on helping him with his garden which he loved, but which was far too much for him to manage alone. Over the years (4-5) we became close friends. I listened to him describe the things going on in his own church and became very aware of his personal spiritual need.

Finally, the day arrived when I felt I must confront the issue of their personal salvation, and I asked their permission to come into their home and specifically talk with them about Christ. They agreed and I did, using the James Kennedy approach. When asked if they wished to receive Christ, they said yes, and prayed to receive Christ. A couple of weeks later I was talking with him and he said, "I have believed in God, and attended church all my life, but, this is the first time it has ever been personal. By then they were in their late eighties, they died about 6 months later, about two weeks apart.

In our weak way we were demonstrating the love of Christ. I believe that over time they began to see God more correctly. God took on flesh through us. Primarily we were servants. I helped him with his garden. No big deal! I enjoy gardening.

As recorded by the Apostle John, the Word became flesh and lived for a while among us. In Jesus, (God had flesh and blood, he walked with man.) God became personal!

Luke records in the Book of Acts these curious words.

"In my former book, Theophilus, I wrote about all that Jesus began to do and teach until the day he was taken up to heaven,"

William Barclay In his commentary, says,

> "......Acts is the second volume of a story which has no end".

The gospel was only the story of what Jesus **began** to do and teach. Jesus earthly life was only the beginning of an activity which has no end."

> Jesus Christ is the exact representation of who God is. He came to this earth to communicate to man who God is.

> But, this was only the first step, this was only the beginning of his attempts to show man who he is and how great His redemptive love is.

When Jesus came to earth he took upon himself human flesh. He was the **WORD** which **BECAME FLESH**

> GOD became a man in the person of Jesus Christ.

When the WORD became flesh, he left behind his divine prerogatives, He was totally dependent upon his relationship with God the father, and his relationship with the Spirit of God for his miraculous power. He was one solitary man, in one place at one time.

Jesus was God, become personal, but because he was only one man, as a man He was limited, as any one man, is limited. As Paul noted "he made himself nothing" Phil. 2:7

As Jesus prepared to leave this earth, he revealed the solution, planned by God; He would not leave them orphans, but would come and be <u>in them</u> through his Spirit. God would <u>multiply himself almost infinitely</u> by indwelling His followers. See John 14:15-21

When Jesus died on the cross, and rose again on the third day his mission as an atoning sacrifice was complete. On God's part reconciliation with man was an accomplished fact.

But, the ministry of reconciliation was just begun.

"JESUS MINISTRY CONTINUES IN US!

NOTICE: JESUS IS STILL ON EARTH

HE IS WORKING THROUGH ME

HE IS WORKING THROUGH YOU!" Garlow, James Lester, <u>Partners in ministry, laity and Pastors working together,</u> Kansas City, MO.: Beacon Hill Press, 1981.

Therefore, if anyone is in Christ, he is a new creation; the old has gone, the new has come! All this is from God, who reconciled us to himself through Christ and <u>gave us the ministry of reconciliation:</u> that God was reconciling the world to himself in Christ, not counting men's sins against them. <u>And he has committed to us the message of reconciliation.</u> We are therefore Christ's ambassadors, as though God were making his appeal through us. II Corinthians 5:17-20a

Jesus specifically, began preparing his disciples for this ministry, as he prepared them for the fact that He himself would be leaving them.

As noted earlier: this preparation is described most clearly in the words of the apostle John in chapters 14-17, Especially, John 14:15-15:17; 16:5-16; 17:2026.

So we return to the church as the **body** of Christ as a description, for our understanding of the nature of the church, and of what we are to do.

Through the Church which is Christ body, Jesus again clothes Himself with human flesh so that he can touch the world through it, with the purpose of reconciling it to Himself.

WHEN, I AM "IN CHRIST" AND "CHRIST IS IN ME", AND I TOUCH ANOTHER PERSON, **CHRIST IS TOUCHING THAT PERSON.**

God in Christ, and in the Church, **is still attempting to make Himself personal!!**

A key element that Jesus emphasized is recorded by John

Jesus is **in** his disciples through the Counselor, or Spirit of truth.

The Holy Spirit is often referred to as Jesus other self.

Jesus purpose from the beginning was to live in us, and for us to live (or have our being) in Him.

But wait a minute, how can this happen? If Jesus is fully human, how can he be inside of me? First, he went away, as he told his first disciples he would. Then He returned in the person of the Holy Spirit. This can happen through a real indwelling of God's Spirit, the Holy Spirit or Christ's other self, living in you or me.

Whether we are aware of His presence or even want His presence, the Holy Spirit is more present with us, than even those persons who are bodily with us, because He knows every thought and intention of our hearts whether good or evil.

When we have received Christ, The Spirit is not only with us, but IN us. The Spirit is in us to encourage, to empower, and to guide.

"When he, The Spirit of truth, comes, he will guide you into all truth. John 16:13

When we yield ourselves to Christ as a vessel for his use, the importance of guidance from the Spirit of truth cannot be over emphasized. First we have a human tendency to self-deception, a tendency of believing half-truths. When being tempted, we are often willing to believe out-right deception by Satan himself. Satan often disguises himself as an angel of light, but who is in fact, the master of lies. Thus it is absolutely essential that we have clear guidance from God's Spirit.

The Christ "in me" and I "in Him Principles

As stated earlier the phrases "in Christ" and "Christ in you," describe the mystical union between Christ and his Church. This union is at the heart of the Church's relationship to Christ as His body.

Here, at this point, we are talking about the means with which Christ continues to have contact with the world through His Spirit.

In Christ

We are to be, "**In Christ**" or, in the Body of Christ (the church) as one of its parts.

First, being "in Christ" means <u>having life.</u> John 15:5-6

Apart from Christ we are totally devoid of life and the ability to produce fruit.

Second, being "in Christ" is the basis for Unity

While the body is diverse even as the human body is diverse, it maintains its unity though its contact with its head, which is Christ.

This is seen in any modern army, it will be effective in its deployment over a large area, only as it maintains contact with and follows the instructions of the commander in chief.

Christ prayed regarding the disciples who would later believe the message of the first disciples.

"That all of them may be one, Father, Just as you're in me and I am in you. May they also be in us so that the world may believe that you have sent me. I have given them the glory that you gave me that they may be one as we are one: I in them and you in me. May they be BROUGHT TO COMPLETE UNITY to let the world know that you sent me and have loved them even as you have loved me. John 17:21-23

This prayer of Christ is one of the already, but not yet answered prayers, as it can be answered with one group at one time, yet awaiting answer for another.

For the Corinthian church it was not yet answered. Apparently there were those at Corinth who though they were "in Christ....... [were] mere infants in Christ..."were not taking their instructions from Christ. Because they were still behaving like" mere men" rather than accepting the headship of Christ, there remained quarreling and division among them.

This quarreling and division certainly is not unusual.

The modern "Christian" world has dealt with the problem by adding yet one more denomination, or separate congregation, or reshuffle among themselves, as persons and families move from one congregation to another.

This has become a blatant problem when trying to give unbelievers a general knowledge of the Christian faith.

Again as stated earlier, the church world today is so split by such a multitude of denominations, each with its own key doctrines, that the average non believer does not see it as diversity of Christian belief, rather, they see each denomination, as a different religion. They see these denominations, not only as separate religions, competing with each other, but, competing with the other world religions.

As I drive across the country even I become confused as I look at all the different names of churches. An amusing one that we use to drive by regularly; The Union Separate Baptist Church. What is that supposed to mean? We made up a rhyme, united we stand, divide we fall, union separate, we are nothing at all.

Without Unity, as "One Faith" The Christian Faith, Churches lose their power to help people believe. Having no idea what to believe, they often, choose not to believe at all.

It is safe to say; **that the body will be fully united when the body is fully surrendered to Christ as its head.** You and I are not responsible for what others do, we can set an example of faith and obedience, as we surrender ourselves to him.

While doctrinal diversity is to be expected, the Church needs to be **fully united around the central truths** of the Christian faith in order to fulfill the central mission of the Church.

Christ in you

Looking at the phrase "in Christ" we were looking primarily at the issue of having life "in Christ" and the Unity of the Church. We now turn again, to the phrase "Christ in you"

One of the clearest Scriptural expressions of this concept in found in Paul's words to the Galatians.

> "I have been crucified with Christ and I no longer live, but Christ lives in me.

The life I live in the body, I live by faith in the Son of God, who loves me and gave Himself for me" (Galatians 2:20)

What is the meaning and significance of Christ living in the believer?

Because Jesus Has promised that he well live in us, if we live in him, it means first that we have a living relationship. A living union between Christ and us. This is primary with God. God created man in his image to have fellowship with him. Sin destroyed that relationship. **God first of all wants fellowship with us**, even as he lives in us, and works through us to draw others into this same fellowship.

This union is at the heart of the Church's relationship to Christ as His body.

It is through the Church as the body of Christ that the kingdom of God is here and now, present in the world.

As the body of Christ, not only is the Church presently part of the kingdom of God which has already broken into the kingdoms of this world, **but through His body, the Church, Christ is present in this world to finish His work.**

It is God's purpose to be **in** the world through the Church.

The Church does not exist for itself.

In fact, it does not exist for God Alone.

It exists as God's chosen instrument to bring the world back to God Himself.

As the body of Christ, it exists to make Him known!!!!!!

"Incarnational theology means this— when we reach out and touch other people, It is not we who actually touch, but Christ who touches through us." Garlow, James Lester, Partners in ministry, laity and Pastors working together, Kansas City, MO.: Beacon Hill Press, 1981.

"Where is Jesus Christ at work in our world? How does He touch the problems of society in this twentieth century? The answer is that He is at work exactly as he was at work in His lifetime on earth, doing precisely the same thing. In the days of His flesh He did work through one solitary, earthly, physical body. He is doing the same work now through a corporate, complex body which exists around the world and permeates and penetrates every level of society. It is called the church, the body of

Christ, but its ministry is to the same race Jesus ministered to, under the same basic conditions, facing the same attitudes, and problems. Stedman, Ray c. Body life, Glendale, CA: regal Books 1972. Page 99

What "in the world" are we to do?

We are to live "in Christ" that His life will truly be in us and empower us, that submission to His Lordship and leadership in our lives will enable unity with other believers, in order that those around us may believe.

We are to allow Christ to live in us, such that when we touch others, it may truly be an occasion when Christ is touching others through us.

As Pastor Randy Youngblood in Arizona suggested we pray:

"Make yourself conspicuous in me, O Lord".

Discussion Questions:

For practical reasons of ministry to people; why did Jesus return to heaven?

In practical ways what are some of the ways that Christ might be seen in me?

What is the difference between Christ being seen in me and pointing to myself that people would see how great a person I am?

Where does the role of servant fit?

If a person refuses obedience to Christ as the head of His body, what can this be compared with in the human body?

How important do you believe having God, touch us personally is? How important, to you personally? How important to people in your sphere of influence?

What has the unity of the Church, or the lack thereof meant to you personally?

Crucified with Christ, speaks of death to self. What does that imply in sharing our faith?

Do you personally know anyone who has come to faith in Christ, without someone in some way to point the way?

Creating An Attractive Atmosphere For The Gospel

While I was pastoring a Church in Muskegon, MI, I grew a large garden. It was large in several ways, both its actual size, and the variety and number of plants. The soil was very sandy with little humus. One of the items we grew was tomatoes. While some types of plants would not produce their fruit, my tomatoes did very well, I thought! Planting three dozen plants each year, we harvested enough for the table and a few to can for the winter.

I thought my tomatoes did very well until I got to Lafayette, IN with its rich deep soil. A lady in our church offered me tomato plants. She was shocked by my request for three dozen. Not understanding the differences in the two areas, I still requested and planted three dozen. They grew so large and heavy that inside the fencing I provided to keep them off the ground they grew to 5' tall. We had so many tomatoes not only could we not use them, I couldn't give them all away.

My first year in Custer, SD, I managed to get a few small green tomatoes. I harvested no ripe tomatoes. The soil and the climate don't cooperate. Obviously, both the soil and the climate in Lafayette is most conducive to grow tomatoes.

What kind of soil and climate is most conducive to encourage faith in Jesus Christ in those persons in the community surrounding us as an individual and in the local church community of which we are a part?

For God so <u>loved</u> the world that He <u>gave</u>.

Given this love God has demonstrated, can you imagine any attitude, other than love, with which one would attempt to share with another human being the love that God has and now demonstrates to us?

When I quickly examine myself, I think that at the center of my being I find love. However when I allow God's Spirit to show me myself I also find other sinful motivations, such as pride, self-righteousness, condescension, etc. This demands the constant activity on our part of placing ourselves in the cleansing stream of his blood, and renewed submission to his Spirit.

What is possible in my own strength, will often be light years away from letting Christ love through me. It is only as we fully realize this and ask and receive his supernatural strength, day to day that genuine love begins to happen.

The reality of our Christian experience is tested when we begin real interaction with real people.

Through the years in an attempt to help various relatives we have loaned them money. Seeing a need we tried to respond with love. This act can easily have unintended consequences, especially if you are unprepared to never receive the money back and have a very tight budget. (Lesson: Don't loan money to relatives; instead, give it to them graciously, if appropriate.)

Not being repaid was normally the situation in our case. This at times seriously jeopardized our situation. This easily produces a judgmental attitude, an unforgiving spirit which can easily result in unloving actions. I have had to ask for forgiveness and grace to overcome all of the above sinful attitudes. I often think with shame at how long it usually took me.

Yet it is here in the arena of our attempting to love our neighbor that we will discover whether we will love unconditionally, whether we will minister to the whole person, or just go through the motions. It is here that we will discover whether we will work in the strength of the flesh and motivated by lesser impulses as we use our own natural abilities to achieve some social goal, or if we will work in the strength of the Spirit.

Since we all come to God through Jesus, with our own sinful baggage, at best growing, but not yet mature, this is a process that we must go through as we learn to walk with Him.

The difference is whether one is <u>motivated by love</u> poured into the heart by the Holy Spirit (Rom.5:5), and <u>working through gifts</u> that have been given by this <u>same</u> Holy Spirit; or if we are motivated by our own values, and working in our own strength. The line between the two is often so easily mistaken, that it is only when checked by the Spirit, that we see the difference. Faith that is not maintained, day to day, often becomes fake.

Adam

Adam has to be one of the more interesting characters with whom God in His grace has allowed me to intersect. We came into contact when I was renovating a building in a historic area along one of the routes through to the town near where we lived at that time One afternoon a man on a bicycle with a bundle of clothes came to the door. He indicated that he was a homeless alcoholic, was traveling south to warmer climate for the winter, and wanted a few days' work, so that he could buy food (and drink) as he traveled south.

I was just getting started on a 6-8 month project, and I had plenty of unskilled work needing to be done. I was interested in people; I could always send him on his way later, so I agreed. I didn't know what he did, or where he went after work, but he always was there in the morning, so work he did. A couple of weeks later he approached me and told me that he really liked working with my son and I, as well as with our crew, would I be willing to keep him on? He had done a reasonable job, so I agreed.

Things went well until one morning he did not show up for work; I was concerned about what happened, but having no way to contact him had to let it go. I few days later he came back and explained that he had been camping along the river near by, and had been jailed as a vagrant. After another time or two of this, and my verification of what was happening, I knew something had to change.

The large storage building on my property was kept heated above freezing; it had a bathroom and running water. The flat surface on the wood stove would serve as a cooking surface, and there were salvage refrigerators in the building from apartment use. I offered to set up a mattress in the corner if he wanted to stay there. He spent the winter in the garage.

Adam in no sense became a part of the family, he kept primarily to himself, and we to ourselves, however, there was plenty of time for Adam to watch our family lifestyle, he saw us at our best, and he was there during plenty of negative moments. These interactions were the setting in which brief as well as longer conversations took place. We discussed the impact of Christ in a person's life. We discussed whether it was possible to end his alcohol abuse. We discussed his separation from family. Adam made his first contact with his family in about 15 years. With the volunteer help of a recovered alcoholic physician, he made an aborted attempt get off alcohol, aborted at least in part because; he was so independent that he refused help and attempted to do it cold turkey. I watched him go through DT's and beyond without any assistance, only to fall back after a few weeks. The renewed drinking was worse and I finally had to let him go because he had become unsafe on the job site.

While I admit to plenty of faults as a person, and as a Christian, I believe that I did genuinely love Adam throughout my time with him. I believe that Adam stayed on because he sensed love and respect for him as a person. While during my time with him he never received Christ. I believe that he had an atmosphere in which he could. I also believe that he left in a condition where God could continue working and perhaps later he would experience the miracle of God's grace.

I do not at all suggest this is a model for everyone's involvement with the homeless or other similar persons. At that point in my life, I had a unique situation, I had both the means, and the place. This was also, what I felt God would have me do.

I have determined that if and when I encounter persons in need, if I become involved at all, I will at least take the time to acknowledge them as a person, and have some kind of real personal contact.

Challenge!

Memorize this passage.

"If I speak in the tongues of men and of angels, but have not love, I am only a resounding gong or a clanging cymbal. If I have a gift of prophecy and can fathom all mysteries and all knowledge, and if I have a faith that can move mountains, but have not love, I am nothing. If I give all I possess to the poor and surrender my body to the flames, but I have not love, I gain nothing. I cor. 13:1-3

Love is the foundation, the center, and the circumference of an attractive atmosphere for the gospel,

The following are some of its detractors, as well as other issues that define it.

There are Four <u>Cardinal sins</u> we need to <u>AVOID.</u> When these sins are present the spread of good news regarding Jesus Christ cannot flourish, and may well be stopped entirely.

First, we need to Avoid Hypocrisy:

(Ask the group to write a definition of Hypocrisy to share)

Religious Externalism'

Ritual without reality,

Motion without meaning,

To speak from under a mask,

Someone who is a phony,

someone who says one thing and

does something else.

We are not speaking here of the imperfections of life, even life as a Christian,

We are not speaking of,

Sins of ignorance,

Or sins of weakness

We are speaking of pretending that we are something, or someone, we know we are not.

We are speaking here of the absolute necessity of <u>genuineness</u> if our witness is to be credible.

Mistakes and weaknesses need to be admitted.

Sins need to be confessed and forgiven.

We do not sin, God Forbid, to be forgiven, however, sometimes, and with some people, confession of sin, not only is an expression of genuineness, but may be used of God not only to bring grace to our own life, but may be a means of grace in their life. If we have sinned we must prayerfully consider whether it needs to be confessed not only to God, but to the others involved.

We do need to carefully consider whether this confession will be damaging to others, and certainly to be avoided if done only to make us feel good or look pious.

God told the apostle Paul, "My grace is sufficient for you, for my power is made perfect in weakness." II Cor. 12:9.

Paul Brand speaks of the difference between the crayfish or Lobster family; and the human family. The crayfish wears it skeleton on the outside; the human wears its skeleton on the inside. The difference is immense when we consider our relationship with the world. The exoskeleton provides protection, but growth is difficult, movement is limited, contact with the outside world is uncomfortable. Consider shaking hands with a lobster. The interior skeleton can grow as we grow, it provides freedom of movement. A human feels soft, warm, and responsive.

Much hypocrisy stems from Legalism: attempting to satisfy God by keeping rules. It leads to hypocrisy because it is impossible to accomplish. Even at its best it is a severe limit because it is so far inferior to a real relationship with God, even one that is full of faults and failure.

Keeping rules even when with good intention and as part of our own self-discipline, should be part of our interior life, not part of our exterior life. God's laws are mean to be a schoolmaster, to enable us to learn, to enable the body of Christ to move effectively in its work, not a ladder to God; they are meant to be an interior structure covered with flesh and skin wherein we touch the world with love and compassion. Ideas influenced by Paul Brand Fearfully and Wonderfully Made, A Surgeon Looks at the Human and Spiritual Body, Grand Rapids, MI Zondervan Publishing house, 1980 Chap. 13

Pride is also a major factor leading to hypocrisy, when we fail to achieve in our own strength, it is so easy to pretend rather that admit to God and others our need and receive grace. However, if we come to understand correctly our relationship with God we will flee to him and allow him to make the correctives needed as we live in and with Him.

Second, we need to avoid Rationalism

Rationalism: Noun—the principle or habit of accepting reason as the supreme authority in matters of opinion, belief, or conduct. Theology— The doctrine that human reason, unaided by divine revelation, is an adequate or the sole guide to all attainable religious truth.

The term portrays a person who has no vision of the sovereignty and providence of God. God is not viewed as a living reality, current and interacting in life today.

This person is incapable of seeing what God alone can do in the life of another person. Rationalism reduces the Christian faith to human controlled routines.

Conversion is not a process of human manipulation, but rather of divine transformation. The rationalist is not really capable of seeing this possibility. They are not capable of dreaming God sized goals. Converts if any will be made in their own unholy likeness.

Christianity is viewed through eyes that see little in anything beyond what may be perceived through our human senses.

Such a philosophy siphons away the divine dimensions of life and reduces Christianity to nothing more than glorified humanism.

Persons who think logically, who struggle with faith in the dimension of the unseen, may be tempted toward this even when they cannot define it. Worse the church frequently is only going through the motions of religious behavior. Many thus involved in the routines of the institutional church would vehemently deny this belief system while in practice, living it day to day.

Many institutional churches appear to fit into this category. There often is truth presented, yet it is presented without any obvious living faith. There is no expectation or conviction presented that God is and will act. Under these circumstances, reception of faith, new faith in the lives of others is unlikely.

Third, we need to avoid Impurity

"it is God's will that you should be holy; that you should avoid sexual immorality; That each of you should learn to control his own body in a way that is holy and honorable...... for God did not call us to be impure, but to live a holy life" (I Thessalonians 4:3-4, 7).

When a politician comes under the spotlight for sexual immorality, even though acceptable if kept in secret, that politician can quickly be swept from power.

How much more deadly is the sting of immorality in the life of a believer in canceling all credibility as a witness for Christ?

Jim Baker states:

"There are many answers to the question *'where did things go wrong?'* and one answer is my much-publicized encounter with Jessica Haln. I knew I was wrong the moment I stepped through the door into room 538 at the Sheraton San Key Resort in Clearwater Beach, Florida, on December 6, 1980. I never dream, however, how much trouble opening that door would cause." Jim Baker, I was Wrong. P. 13

The wrong that he did that day was multiplied by the years of secrecy and cover up that followed. Hypocrisy on his part and the part of other leaders destroyed a ministry that though perhaps misguided, had some value in the kingdom. The damage rippled out from there to affect the conscious and subconscious attitudes of the nation and beyond, toward Christianity.

We may think we can hide our sin. When we do so we are only fooling ourselves. Our impact may not be on a nation and beyond as with Jim Baker, but it will have an effect on our family, friends and those in our circle of influence and it will never be good.

Fourth, we need to avoid Legalism

Legalism is an ethical system which measures spirituality in terms of one's compliance with an arbitrary set of rules

The book of Galatians is the book that says the most about this subject. What it says is quite forceful.

For example:

You who are trying to be justified by law have been alienated from Christ; you have fallen away from grace. But by faith we eagerly await through the Spirit the righteousness for which we hope. For in Christ Jesus neither circumcision

nor uncircumcision has any value. The only thing that counts is faith expressing itself through love. Galatians 5 4-6

We cannot be saved by works. The Law was given as a schoolmaster to bring us to Christ.

Legalism not only does not work because we can never attain righteousness through it, but it runs counter to everything God is attempting to establish in a love relationship through faith, and through His Son Jesus Christ.

Over time virtually every individual and group develops, whether written or unwritten, a standard of conduct that characterize them and by which admittance to their inner circle is decided. This has its rightful place; however, there is a place within the love of Christ, where everyone is accepted, because of His grace. We must constantly be seeking to live in that place both for ourselves and those around us.

Even obedience must be properly understood in this discussion. It must not be understood in the context of simply keeping rule. It must be understood in the context of a love relationship with God, through His Son Jesus Christ. It must be understood in the context of doing what God tells me to do, because I fully trust Him and am willing to do what he tells me even when I do not yet fully understand.

Obedience is a faith response. Keeping rules is a works, or self-effort response, one of attempting to earn one's acceptance, and standing. Obedience results from Love and commitment, and brings life. Legalism results in death because it stems from pride.

Our job is not to introduce people to rules for living successfully and getting to heaven. We must introduce people to Jesus Christ, the son of God. In him and him alone is there life. Jesus came that we might know, experientially know God in all his splendor.

A Loving Climate

Contrast the following situations: you were a person in need of food on Thanksgiving Day. One, someone gives you a gift certificate and says, "Here take this and go to McDonalds." Two, someone says, "Let me pick you up at 11, I want you to join me at My Big Fat Greek restaurant where my family and I have a room set aside for the meal."

Evangelism is most effective when based on, and permeated with, love and caring.

Christians are called,

> Christians are spirit filled, to be representatives of Christ Himself;
> and **Christ's most dominate characteristic is love.**

> The Church is quick to agree that we need love.

> Yet the church is often just as slow to embrace the responsibility and costliness of love itself.

Love, as defined by Scripture (I Corinthians 13:4-6) and demonstrated by Jesus Christ, is sacrificial, self-giving love. This kind of love cannot be expressed as a noun, but rather must be described by verbs, or action words.

This love is known by a person's behavior. This love is not natural to "mere men" but rather, this love is poured by the Holy Spirit into the hearts of believers who by faith surrender themselves to God.

A loving climate is one in which there is total acceptance of others as persons regardless of their circumstances or behavior. It relates to an experience of the heart, in which we see people, not just by what they are at the moment, but rather through the eyes of Jesus. It sees people by what they can be by the grace of God. It is a climate where we do not try to force people to conform to our perceived image, but rather where each individual has freedom to become the person God intends him or her to be.

This kind of climate does not happen easily or automatically, rather it's created as believers yield themselves totally to the Spirit of God. It is developed as in honesty persons continually relate to one another within the body of Christ. An increase of this kind of love should be continually encouraged by its demonstration, by the more mature Christians to those who are newer and or less mature in the faith.

This climate of love is not an atmosphere of continual criticism in the name of honesty, rather it is one in which one's own faults are readily acknowledged and forgiveness is sought and given. It is an atmosphere in which criticism, when needed, is given with a continual concern for the person criticized. Sacrificial love is love which dares to confront, but it never confronts out of selfish interests, but rather out of concern for the person confronted, as well as concern for others involved.

Close involvement in small groups gives opportunity for individual Christians to experience love from others, practice love for others, and develop an ability to love wisely. <u>Love needs to be a reality first of all within the Christian community, but it must not end there.</u> The Scriptures clearly indicate the necessity of our love going beyond those who return it to us (Matt. 5:43-48).

The Scriptures reveal that we demonstrate our love for God, by our love for others.

In fact,

Our actions toward others are identified as actions toward God Himself.

"For I was hungry and you gave me something to eat, I was thirsty and you gave me something to drink, I was a stranger and you invited me in, I needed clothes and you clothed me, I was sick and you looked after me, I was in prison and you came to visit me."

Then the righteous will answer him, "Lord, when did we see you hungry and feed you, or thirsty and give you something to drink? When did we see you a stranger and invite you in, or needing clothes and cloth you? When did we see you sick or in prison and go visit you?"

The King will reply, "I tell you the truth, whatever you did for one of the least of these my brothers of mine, you did for me" (Matt. 25:35-40).

These words of Jesus ought not to be seen as a legalistic requirement for getting to heaven, rather as a clear picture of what it looks like in action to love God with all our heart and our neighbor as our self. It shows an expression of genuine faith.

It becomes obvious as we comprehend the meaning of Jesus words that love involves far more than simply an occasional emotional response.

True love for Christ, and thus for others, Means

"a basic, down –to—earth involvement with people in need. The response is to be personal …. The response is to be caring. The people….may not require clothing, food, or water. *But they do have real needs.* Responding to the void of loneliness, frustration or despair demands a personal investment of genuine caring. Emphasis mine. Arn, Win, The Master's Plan for Making Disciples, Pasadena, CA: Church Growth Press,1962 P.99.

"The first, and most important role of sharing our faith, and a role that anyone can fulfill, is that of love and caring. When everyone in the Christian community becomes involved in ministry at this level it produces and atmosphere in which verbal witness becomes effective." John W. Mowat, The Ministry of the Laity in its Social Contact and its effect on Evangelism, 1983 Grace is the dominate gift of God to man flowing from His love.

In all of the circumstances we find men in, as they confront their sin and its pain, knowing of God's grace, by seeing our graciousness to them, is an absolute essential to them seeing Christ in us.

Discussion Questions

When thinking of the Church as the Body of Christ, which parts of the body should be in contact with the world, its skin, or its bones? Why? What is the primary purpose of skin, of bones?

What facts does a person need to grapple with to become a disciplined, devoted follower?

When the "world" encounters the Body of Christ in the work day world, what is its appearance, its texture, its feel?

How does Hypocrisy in our lives and/or the lives of others affect people we are trying to witness to?

How does Impurity in our lives and/or the lives of others affect people we are trying to witness to?

What kind of activities can the Church be involved in that show love on a personal basis to unbelievers?

What kind of activities can I be involved in that show love on a personal basis to unbelievers?

Who needs love the most, down and outers, or up and outers?

Under what circumstances am I most likely to be able to show love to a down and outer, to an up an outer?

Who are you already most in contact with?

What activities should I become involved with, or more involved with, what activities should I quit, strictly from an evangelistic perspective?

When viewed from the perspective of demonstrating love personally, what outreach activities of the church should be encouraged?

Getting to know unbelievers

The art of listening

It was my first Church. I was young and still ignorant of some of the basics of electricity and electrical wiring. The parsonage was furnished with a very old electric dryer. It worked fine and we used it for a couple of years until one day it quit and nothing I could do seemed to get it going. The light still worked so I knew it was getting power. It was old so repair seemed to be a foolish waste of money. We went out and bought a new electric dryer.

When we got the new dryer home and all hooked up, we turned it on only to discover that it behaved just like the old one. The light would come on, but he dryer would not operate. Needless to say, we had a different problem. No one seemed to know what to suggest until I talked to a savvy lady business owner who asked me if I had checked the 220 fuses. Sure enough, one was defective. I was getting 110 power to the dryer which operated the light, but did not have the 220 power required for the dryer itself.

My ignorance cost me a dryer, which I would not have needed to purchase, but which because it was mine, went with me and served us well for many years.

Many, well-meaning Christ sharers, make similar mistakes of ignorance that could easily be avoided if they would learn to do one very simple thing.

Listen

I was astounded when I read an article in the March 2014 Reader Digest entitled <u>The Psychic, the Novelist, and the $17 Million Scam</u> to discover just how badly some feel the need for someone to listen.

This article relates the story that came out in the court proceedings when Rose Marks, a grandmother in her 60's, a psychic in Manhattan was charged and found guilty of bilking novelist Jude Deveraux, whose books have sold some 60 million copies, out of more than 17 million of her profits. This all started relatively small. How did it continue and escalate to the extent of 17 million?

"I kept coming back because she was listening to me. I've never been able to get anyone to listen to me," Deveraux testifies"

What would have happened if a Christian associate, neighbor or friend had taken the time to really listen? Who are the persons around you who are desperate for someone to really listen?

Yes! We want to share what Christ means in our lives.

<u>BUT</u>

<u>Before sharing our own story, it is absolutely critical that we discover their story.</u>

In order to discover their story, we must **learn to listen**.

The consequence of not listening, are far ranging.

Even though we may care greatly, we may come across as being only interested in our own agenda and not caring at all about the other person.

Or, we may be answering questions that they have not yet asked themselves and leave them in total confusion.

Or, we may be attempting to persuade them to accept Christ, when they have no clue who He is, where He lives, or why they should not start "saving" just like he does.

Or, worse, we may totally miss the times when verbal and none verbal cues indicate that our friend has a very significant area of felt need, and we go on about life as if absolutely nothing is going on beyond sports, the latest fashion, and our ingrown toe nail. To miss these types of cues is at best, to perhaps miss an opportunity to show love. At worst we may have missed an opportunity to introduce them to the one who can meet their need.

I find myself constantly confronting situations when afterward I wish I had been a better listener. My need to be heard, my agenda, my lack of thoughtfulness of the other person, are all reasons for being distracted, forgetful and experience the need for the check of God' s Spirit.

<u>Very few people are good listeners.</u>

We are poor listeners with good reason.

While writing is least used, - - - it is most taught.

Speaking is next used and it is next taught.

<u>Listening is most used, but-----it is least taught.</u>

Therefore:

We must learn how to listen,

And we must unlearn poor listening habits.

Some Problem areas we need to be aware of are:

1. Thoughts and feelings are difficult to verbalize.
    Consequently, thoughts and feelings may be unclearly expressed.
    If we have not learned to listen carefully, we may hurry on without understanding.

    Think of those times when there was a very important, perhaps very painful, issue you needed to speak to another about. It is at those very times when it becomes most difficult to begin speaking, or to clearly express what you feel.

I am personally acquainted with an individual that confessed to me that it took well over a week to begin to talk with individuals that were respected and trusted about a situation that was so painful and so overwhelming that he could hardly function. A person busy with their own agenda would most likely miss totally any opportunity to minister. If this person began to speak and felt that they were not being heard, they most likely would quit and not restart.

2. Identification and squishy spots. We need to guard carefully against reading into their situation, our own past or present problems, and trying to make our solution their solution.

3. Jumping to <u>cause</u> and jumping to <u>conclusions.</u>
   Listen, listen, listen, you are not necessarily meant to identify either cause of conclusion rather to allow God to show them what is important.

4. Perceptions and experience differ.
   Examples
   Hindu vs. Christian cultures
   Wealth vs. poverty
   Raised in church vs. no religious training.
   Black vs. White

5. Our minds wander.
6. Lack of patience
7. Lack of time.
8. Feelings of being overwhelmed

I personally tend to jumping in too quick, whether to tell my own story, or to solve their problem.

Principles of Active Listening

As you focus on the principles of active listening.

   Remember,

   The purpose of listening is to accurately discover their story.

      Their story

         is not just a

      religious story.

      It is who they are,

         Especially the significant highs and lows of their Life,

            from their perspective.

      Love makes you interested in them! <u>Period.</u>

The desire to share Christ makes you **especially** interested in (1.) where they are in their spiritual journey. (2.) What their past and present felt needs are as related to what Christ offers to them.

However,

<u>Genuine love makes you interested in them unconditionally regardless of their response.</u> It makes you interested in them as a whole person, not just their religious response.

Active listening.....

......is a skill which can be learned.

......builds trust and relationship.

......means allowing the speaker time to tell you what he/she wants you to know.

......means being able to discern what the speaker is wanting: action, Information, etc.

> IE, you will begin to know whether they are ready to take the next step, need more information for a basis for another step, or perhaps want you to back off and leave them alone.

......shows respect for the speaker.

> In the action of actively listening you do not place value judgments on what has been told to you. You may not agree but the person is still worthy of respect. It is not our role to act as judge and jury. Christ Himself when confronted with the woman caught in adultery did not condemn her, rather sent her away to sin no more. The Holy Spirit Himself will point out our quilt.

......means that you are a facilitator of the speaker's exploration of himself/herself.

> You are not a problem solver. Time may come for this at some point, but not until you have first listened. Even then, Christ is the problem solver; you are effective only through Him

......means being able accurately to "mirror" back to the speaker his/her own feelings.

> Mirroring is repeating back to a person (using different words) what you believe they have said, the emotion you understand they are expressing, as well as the content. Mirroring allows you to be sure you have understood what they have said; it slows down the process allowing for additional thought, and sometimes adds insight for the other person. It also assures the speaker that you are listening. You are both on the same page!

......helps the speaker explore his/her own choices, feelings, and behaviors-**not yours.**

> We are always so prone to put ourselves in the center. Really actively listening, keeps the conversation, other centered.

Active listening to another's struggles will aid you in your own growth if you allow it to happen.

LISTENING: If you find speaking the words of the gospel difficult, you may be especially gifted at listening. Introverts may have natural gifts in this area that are very difficult for extroverts. This does not excuse the extrovert for being a poor listener, just acknowledges their obstacles. Many times, really listening, with few if any allusions to "Faith solutions"; may enable the baby steps that God can use to move your friend from their stance of resistance, or indifference, to a more direct response to God.

Nancy Ortberg of Menlo Park Presbyterian Church in Menlo, California, was quoted in a Forbes article on Godly Work. In her sermon, "Jesus and Your Job" she said "No matter what your job is you have an opportunity to live that out" (your faith) "every day. Work gives you an opportunity to make a meaningful and significant contribution to the world. Unlike being in church, work gives you an opportunity to live out what it means when Jesus says, 'You are salt, and you are light.'"

During a time when she was an emergency room nurse she observed the following:

"It was about 10:30 p.m. The room was a mess. I was finishing up some work on the chart before going home. The doctor with whom I loved working, was debriefing a new doctor, who had done a very respectable, competent job, telling him what he'd done well and what he could have done differently.

"Then he put his hand on the young doctor's shoulder and said, "when you finished, did you notice the young man from housekeeping who came in to clean the room?' There was a completely blank look on the young doctor's face.

The older doctor said, 'his name is Carlos. He's been here for three years. He does a fabulous job. When he comes in, he gets the room turned around so fast that you and I can get our next patients in quickly. His wife's name is Maria. They have four children". Then he named each of the four children and gave each child's age.

"The older doctor went on to say, 'He lives in a rented house about three blocks from here, in Santa Ana. They've been up from Mexico for about five years. His name is Carlos', he repeated. Then he said, "Next week I would like you to tell me something about Carlos that I don't already know. Okay? Now let's go check the rest of the patients." Forbes, April 27, 07 Godly work, Page 27

This article was emphasizing leadership and the example excels, but to me is a powerful example of listening and caring.

Useful questions in getting to know people

This section is perhaps presumptive since each individual is unique whether the believer or unbeliever, however in the attempt to get you thinking and perhaps prime the pump as was often necessary with the old hand pumps prior to electricity, we will make an attempt.

Some guidelines are in order.

First, this is primarily an opportunity to listen, not a time to show you superior knowledge.

Second, questions probably should differ when speaking to old acquaintances' vs. new acquaintances', though if it relates to areas never discussed that might not be true.

Third, questions are rarely appropriate if we in reality, are not prepared to listen. Questions are not appropriate unless we are truly trying to understand a person, their values, their ideas, who and why they are the person they are.

Fourth, I doubt that questions are ever valid if they are only a platform from which to launch our own opinions and beliefs.

1. Questions about life in general, especially when they relate to caring about events in another's life that produce change. These questions may relate to current events in their family life. They may relate to what they do in their spare time, hobbies, etc. Questions may relate to their family, even their family of origin. They may relate to their work, past, present, and future dreams or goals.

    Questions related to where they have lived, the type of neighborhood, where they have traveled, vacationed will give insight into what they thing and believe and why? For example someone who was raised as an Army brat, and who has lived all over the world, often separate for long periods of time will have a very different view of life from one who has lived in the same neighborhood all their life.

2. Casual ice breaker type questions:

    What's the most exiting / memorable thing you have ever done?

    What would you do if you had more spare time?

3. Questions designed to make a person think and give you insight into their thoughts. For example:

    > If you were God how would you deal with (some life situation of common interest)?

    > Do you ever have trouble finding live meaningful?

    > What do you think is the underlying cause of the unrest in our neighborhood?

Do you really feel Loved? Do you feel (any number of things?) Do you believe in anything you cannot prove? Why?

How do you figure out what is true, Right, Moral, etc.?

John was 70, had lived in a truck or VW camper for over 40 years, I already knew he was agnostic, that he believed God was an evil God. I knew he had read widely regarding world religions, including repeated readings of the bible.

We had a good start on the evening meal for two guests when we had a cancelation due to an injury in a fall. I had already been contemplating whether further conversation with John was appropriate or possible. At the last minute, I invited him to eat the meal with us. He accepted. After the meal, knowing his strong views and potential openness to dialogue I ask him, "do you consider yourself as searching for truth, or do you believe you have found". He gave a yes and no answer. I listened for 45 minutes with no response other than questions to clarify his thinking.

Because he had valid questions that deserved answers and thoughtful observations regarding scripture, I complimented him on this and entered dialogue to answer critical questions he had asked. I encouraged him to reread the gospel of John looking for Jesus declaration of who he is and whether that could be true. He left indicating he would read John and get back with me.

John was thinking new thoughts when he left with an openness to further dialogue.

4. Questions based on your observations:

Have you ever thought about why you seldom seem happy?

Have you ever thought about why you are always angry?

You don't seem to need the money, but you seem compelled to always be working. You ever wonder why?

What just happened did not seem that big a deal to the others involved, do you know what makes you feel so strongly?

The only dependable way to know how, and what questions to ask is to respond to the leadings of the Spirit of God. If you have already listened to your friend, tuned in to the wisdom that comes from God, this will give you clues as to what questions will be helpful and can be used of God. I am not aware of ever having chosen ahead of time what questions I would ask. I have tried to be sensitive to both God and the person I am with. Yet honest questions over time, used when the right occasions arise can be used of God to unlock doors of the heart.

Listen, make appropriate comments and follow up questions. Share a little of yourself and your story if appropriate. This will help keep these times natural and not seem like you are grilling them. If this is truly someone you love and care about you do not want it to be.

Discussion

As you think back on your own journey toward God, who is the main person who reached out to you? Describe the way this person listened, loved, reached out to you?

The willingness to walk across the room to a complete stranger is often incredibly important. But, what about those persons God has already placed next to you?

What if you ---do not even need to walk across the room--- What if people are already in your circle of contacts, or web of relationships? What advantage do you have in building a relationship over a period of time?

Think about your present sphere of influence—including where you live, where you work, the people in your small group, your friends, your relatives, your acquaintances and so on. How do you think God expects *your* specific evangelistic style to impact the lives of these people?

What do you currently know of the stories of those in your sphere of influence?

What does this motivate you to learn?

How does it motivate you to pray?

What ideas do you have at this point that will "make Christ conspicuous in your life" to those who are already in your web of relationships? How is listening, a part of making Christ conspicuous in your life?

Action Groups

Divide into groups of two to three persons. Let each person take not more than 5 minutes (check your watch) to tell their, before and after conversion story. What were your felt needs? How and through whom did you learn enough to first come to Faith? What did you discover in the Gospel story that met your need? (Perhaps as observed first in someone else's life) What issue's brought you to faith?

The most critical question, <u>what difference has Christ really made in your life?</u> What changes took place in your life immediately? What changes have taken place more gradually?

Other group members are to be practicing active listening. Try to really listen. Take brief notes to give immediately, to the story teller for their assistance in later writing out their own story. Avoid interruption except as really essential to understand what they are expressing both in words and feeling. If you are clarifying an issue, attempt to use mirroring both for practice and to help you understand.

Characteristics of Unbelievers

Expect unbelievers to be and act like sinners. Christ, said; "I have not come to call the righteous, but sinners. Matt. 9:13 It is not necessarily easy to love people with sometimes, hateful behavior and attitudes, and with whom we have, perhaps constant contact, yet these are the very persons Christ died to save. Without the constant presence of Christ in our lives by the power of His Spirit, It will be **impossible**.

Paul writing to the Church at Corinth, says, "I have become all things to all men so that by all possible means I might save some." I Corinthians 9:22

Paul did this because people were different, and of different backgrounds. Some were raised with the Law; some were raised without the Law, etc.

In the U. S. we still live in a culture which largely has a Christian background. This fact can no longer be assumed to be true of the general population. In fact, it is often untrue.

Even when a person's background is Christian, this background may be so remote as to be meaningless. For many with a Christian background, the most it means is that they do not have some other background.

Almost universally our U.S. culture is permeated by the teachings found in schools from kindergarten through university, of what I describe as atheistic evolution and accompanying secular humanism. Evolution is generally taught not as an explanation of process of change within a created world of intelligent design, but rather as a substitute for God and supposedly a fully "scientific" explanation of everything.

This results in either an outright rejection of the possibility of God, or living in a dichotomy in which individuals don't know what to believe. In a world in which the Church has for many lost its credibility, this has serious implications and must be addressed in some manner. Faith must be engendered either with such clear life change in us that show forth the Glory of God, or with frank discussion that allows them to see intellectually the reasonableness of faith and make that leap. Hopefully both will be true.

> Increasingly, even in the U.S. we will encounter persons with other religions beliefs,
>
> These beliefs may be ones which they firmly hold, and that they actively practice.
>
> Or, these beliefs may simply be part of their background, and seemingly inconsequential; yet seemingly inconsequential issues, may become major if challenged, especially if challenged thoughtlessly.
>
> Even if these beliefs are only part of their background and not firms held, they may be so subconsciously part of their believe system that they will influence and make new beliefs difficult to take hold.

In addition, we need to consider the media generation in which we live. The average person is bombarded by so many different messages daily, that they could not survive, without selective hearing, selective seeing, and the ability to tune out emotionally those items of which they do not want to be a part.

Thus it is the nature of our society that persons who have not had reason to pay attention to anything related to the Christian faith, will never really see our buildings, read with any comprehension or ads, let alone grasp the meaning of our rhetoric. It is completely off there radar. It is outside their range of hearing.

It is in this context,

that we need to be prepared to share our faith.

The Apostle Paul did not change the gospel to satisfy the different people he encountered, but he did adapt his own personal habits, and the methods with which he presented the gospel. As Paul did not use a generalized approach, we also need to be careful of using a generalized approach.

A vacuum cleaner salesman using a generalized approach would give the standard sales pitch, even if the house had no carpets. He would vacuum the non-existent carpets and clean the non-existent drapes.

After being turned down, he would go next door and repeat the process.

Core central truths remain the same, **motivators** change with people and circumstances.

Look at Jesus' approach to people, their possible **motivation** to follow and the methods he used.

Mark 1:16-20

> Simon and Andrew, James and John, Jesus calls them to follow and he will make them fishers of men. They were motivated to do something with their lives.

Mark 2:13-17

> Levi, a tax collector, Jesus follows him, evidently to Levi's home, where he told the critics that he sought sinners, not the righteous. I think Levi along with all others of this type knew he had need. He felt guilt, he needed forgiveness, and he needed acceptance.

Mark 10:17-26

> The rich young ruler came to Jesus with a question: "what must I <u>do</u> to inherit eternal life?" Knowing that the ruler sought eternal life through, good works, Jesus appealed to an issue of the heart, and required the very thing, that would force him to acknowledge that he could not achieve it on his own.

John 3:1-21

> Nicodemus sought God from a position of religious knowledge, but evidently with emptiness. Jesus reveals Nicodemus' ignorance in the face of knowledge, he showed that real life is of the heart and comes through the power of the Spirit of God.

John 4:4-26

> The Samaritan woman at the well does not even know she is seeking until Christ offers her something she wanted, but beyond her initial ability to comprehend. He follows up by helping her to discover Himself, the source of life and meaning.

John 5:3-15

> The 38 year invalid. "Do you want to get well?" "Get up! Pick up your mat and walk." Jesus required desire and faith sufficient to obey.

As we look at how Jesus approached people, we see that Jesus engaged them as unique individuals. He saw their unique backgrounds and specific areas of felt need.

In the parable of the sower, Mark 4:13-20; Jesus shows some of the characteristics of the unbeliever.

He shows

First, like soil in a pathway, are those who are so quickly blinded by Satan that the truth never takes root in their lives.

Second, like soil on rocky places, are those who receive quickly with little thought, but which because there is no depth of understanding, character, or commitment, just as quickly discard what they have received.

Third, like soil choked by thorns, are those who allow worry (distrust), wealth (trust in things), desire for other things (other things become god) to choke out the truth.

Fourth, those who are like good soil

These characteristics all relate to receptivity once the truth is spoken (word is sown).

Can you relate these soil conditions to People who surround you? Can you relate these soil conditions to your own life at various periods?

As we ponder soil conditions we need to remember that soil conditions need not and do not always remain the same. Pathways sometimes are moved. Rocky soil can be broken up. Weedy, thorny, soil can be cultivated.

There are three different primary areas of concern related to characteristics of the unbeliever to which we need to be alert.

These areas of concern are of paramount importance, because they dictate how and what we should communicated with unbelievers.

First: How much does the unbeliever know?

Expressed in descending order they might be expressed as follows:

-6 No real awareness or acknowledgement of the existence of a supreme being.

-5 Awareness of a supreme being mixed with various religious traditions including the worship of idols. There may be a mix of information that already produces great confusion. Presentation of Christian information sometimes has added to the confusion.

-4   Initial awareness of the Christian tradition. There is no awareness of the basics of Christianity, or of the implications of the gospel.

-3   There is a grasp of the basics of the gospel.

-2   There is a grasp of the implications of the gospel.

-1   There is a personal awareness of problems in their life, and an awareness of need.

0   There is an experiential knowledge of God in the person of Jesus Christ.

Second: What is the unbeliever's Attitude?

Again, expressed in somewhat of a descending order as follows:

-7   Believes that there is no God. Man is king.

-6   Awareness of God but, Judges God to be totally unacceptable, an unjust tyrant, etc.

-5   Awareness of God, but the God they accept is a false god.

-4   Awareness of God, but considers Him to be irrelevant. Example: God made the earth then abandoned it, type attitude.

-3   Awareness of God, but, he cannot be found; at least I cannot find Him.

-2   Positive awareness of God, I am trying to find Him. They may be wrestling with some of the major problem questions.

-1   Actively seeking God. They are reading books about God. They are reading the Bible. Actively talking to others of faith.

Third: What are their felt needs, or, what are their motivators?

Maslow's: Hierarchy of needs

Self-Actualization
Frustration
Emptiness
Uselessness
Boredom
Lack of fulfillment

Self Esteem
Guilt
Failure
Inadequacy
Embarrassment
Lack of recognition

Love / Affection
Loneliness
Anxiety
Fear
Lack of appreciation
Rejection
Isolation
Dejection

Safety/Security
Threatened
Insecurity
Weakness
Tiredness
Sickness

Pain

Physiological
Hunger
Thirst
Shelter

Look carefully at the **I AM** statements of Christ and see how they related to Maslow's hierarchy of needs.

"I who speak to you am he", by inference; I am the Messiah. John 4:26

"I am the bread of life." John 6:35

I am the living water. By implication John 7:38

"I am the light of the world" John 8:12

"I am the one who testifies for myself" John 8:18

"Before Abraham was born, I am". John 8:58

"I am the gate for the sheep." John 10:7

"I am the good shepherd". John 10:11

"I am God's Son". John 10:36

"I am the resurrection and the life". John 11:25

"I am the way and the truth and the life." John 14:6

"I am the true vine." John 15:1

When we look closely at these declarations, all identifying with God's declaration to Moses, I Am that I Am; stating his self-existence, Jesus is not only identifying himself as God but also showing us the nature of God and how he relates to meet our needs and the needs of those who are around us.

God has created us to respond to reward and motivation. Even Christ, the author and perfecter of our faith, endured the cross, for the joy that was set before him. Hebrews 12:3

Need and reward are part of the essence of human existence.

People come to Christ only in response to some area of felt need. They come when their **felt need** couples with faith that Christ can and will meet that need.

The following are characteristic misconceptions of unbelievers.

(Note: they are **all** works related)

"I don't need it" I can earn salvation myself.

"I must improve first." God could not accept me as I am so I will have to get good enough that he will.

"I don't think I can live it." Since it depends on my effort, and I cannot do it, so I will not try.

Where does your friend fit into the salvation by works scenario?

Salvation: "It is the gift of God---not by works, so that no one can boast". Ephesians 2:8-9

In the following case study, note any observations that you have related to getting to know unbelievers and the unique characteristics of each individual.

Sheri

I first met Sheri when I interviewed she, and her husband, when they were looking at an apartment that I owned. I subsequently rented to them for about 4 years, while Bill was working on his Doctorate. They had already lived in the USA for several years on Student visas while pursuing education and involved in the work place. In spite of their outgoing manner and deliberate attempts to not seclude themselves within their own culture, to this point they had never been in a home of a non-east-Indian American, for a meal.

We began occasional visits back in forth, including meals. We discovered the thrill of their Cuisine, and they the enjoyment of the standard basic

European American food that we served. Since, they had no family or friends in the area with which to share the holidays, our family including children and grandchildren, welcomed them as regular guests, to Christmas, Thanksgiving, and other special occasions. Another tenant family from Montana with a different faith also added to the mix.

Yes, religion did play a part in our discussions, as they wanted to know what Christmas, and Christianity was all about. Certainly religion played a part as they share their religion and we shared ours.

I took advantage of those occasions, along with others to listen carefully to their beliefs, and to clarify in my mind the nature of their religion. Again religions were discussed when she described some of the pain of her younger years in their home country. This pain was acute, in spite of parents that loved her, and coming from a relatively wealthy family. Yes, religions were discussed when she shared with tears the fact that as a young adult with no meaning, and a life of emotional pain, she had barely survived attempted suicide. She indicated that I was the first person in the US with whom she had ever shared this part of her life.

These kinds of images were shared in a context in which she knew she was loved, in which she knew that I was really listening and cared about her as a person. They were shared in a context in which I occasionally asked probing questions as I felt it was the right time.

I faced the difficulty then and now, of helping her to distinguish between her belief systems of accepting Jesus Christ, as a prophet, as a god among many, and accepting Him as the only true God, as her Lord and only God.

She accepted Christ, and until they moved months later, regularly attended church with us. They have attended church both in another state and in Canada since their latest move. But old belief and value systems are difficult to break, especially when tied to faith issues connected to things we cannot see. I continue to pray. Visits are few and difficult, but we keep occasional contact by phone and internet.

Discussion questions:

In considering Sheri's story what characteristics of the unbeliever did you identify?

What progression have you become aware of as Sheri's attitude and knowledge changed?

How was active listening demonstrated?

What other principles that we are learning do you see in this story?

What would you have wanted to share with her about Christ?

What issues do you think would need to be discussed?

Viewing one of the persons in your sphere of influence, where do you see them in their attitude toward God at present, what are they currently aware of in their knowledge of God, how much of this is in line with the truth, how much of it relates to misconceptions?

Recognizing responsive People

Jesus recognized <u>un</u>responsive people!

> "O Jerusalem, Jerusalem, you who kill the prophets and stone those sent to you, how often I have longed to gather your children together, as a hen gathers her chicks under her wings, but you were not willing! Look, your house is left to you desolate. I tell you, you will not see me again until you say, 'Blessed is he who comes in the name of the Lord.' ". Luke 13:34-35.

<u>Jesus recognized responsive people!</u>

> Jesus went through all the towns and villages, teaching in their synagogues, preaching the good news of the kingdom and healing every

disease and sickness. When he saw the crowds, he had compassion on them, because they were harassed, and helpless, like sheep without a shepherd. Then he said to his disciples, the harvest is plentiful but the workers are few. Ask the Lord of the harvest, therefore, to send out workers into his harvest field. Matt. 9: 3538

In the last session, we were attempting to recognize and understand both the general characteristics of unbelievers, and to be able to relate that information to specific individuals. We want to know how to relate to them as individuals. It is critical that we know what of our story relates to them, and especially what to share of the gospel story as it relates to their needs.

In this session we are attempting to learn to recognize those times when people are approachable, when they are open to the gospel, when they are likely to listen.

It makes little difference if we know what of our story, or of the gospel story would related to another person's needs, if they have closed hearts and minds and will not listen.

God has made man with the capacity to choose, and while he patiently woos them and attempts to demonstrate His love, he never forces a person to accept. We must learn to work with God, which means we do not push if they are not responsive.

Jesus calls us to minister to responsive people! Jesus confronted people with truth of the gospel, but he never attempted to force unwilling people.

The most effective disciple making plan is to identify receptive people or individuals who God has prepared, and win them while they are winnable.

How then do we identify responsive people?

First, Identify Transition Periods:

"The span of time in which a person's or family's normal everyday behavior patterns are disrupted by an event that puts them in an

unfamiliar situation." Win Arn: <u>The Master's Plan for Making Disciples</u> P. 90
Ibid

Attentive listening will allow us to be aware of times of transition.

Transition times are a particularly important time to stay in touch with those in our sphere of influence, and to respond immediately when we sense, or become aware of openness.

We need to use great care here. While <u>immediate response</u> may be critically important, this is an occasion in which we must be<u> first</u>, ceaseless in prayer, as we ask God how to respond,<u> second</u>, we must be attentively listening to gain the clues as to how God is already working, and how they are responding. Is their attitude changing, for the better, for the worse? Is a worse attitude bluster? <u>Third,</u> we need to be attentive to the leadership of the Holy Spirit as to our next steps.

Does God want us to just be a friend and listen, allowing them to gain insight by just being able to talk it out without judgment or advice? Does God want us to show love by some kind of appropriate action? Is this the time for sharing all or part of my story, all or part of God's story? Are there others in the body of Christ who should be involved NOW, perhaps a person with unique gifts and connection to this situation?

The answer to these questions is related to where they are in their knowledge of God, where they are in their attitude toward God, strength of their felt need, the strength or weakness of our relationship with them, and certainly the leadership of God's Spirit for this time and place.

The more recent and disruptive, the event, or circumstance in a person's life, the more likely it is, that he or she will be open to a new lifestyle which includes Christ and the church.

It is important to recognize that: <u>a person can be totally ignorant of God, they</u> <u>may be totally resistant, but with a change of circumstances,</u> <u>they may become</u> <u>responsive to the gospel.</u>

Win Arn in <u>The Master's Plan for Making Disciples,</u> gives a list of events which may result in transition periods in the life of an individual or family. The higher the number given the more disruptive and possible transition producing for some significant change in lifestyle; the more likely they may be open to responding to God in their life. If there are more than one event taking place at the same time, it increases the likely hood of change.

Death of a spouse	100
Divorce	73
Marital separation	65
Jail time	63
Death of a close family member	63
Personal injury or illness	53
Marriage	50
Fired from work	47
Marital reconciliation	45
Retirement	45
Change in family members health	45
Pregnancy	40
Sex difficulty	39
Addition to family	39
Business readjustment	39
Change in financial status	38
Death of a close friend	37
Change in number of marital arguments	35
Mortgage or loan over $10,000	31
Foreclosure of Mortgage or loan	30
Change in work responsibilities	29
Son or daughter leaving home	29
Trouble with in laws	29
Outstanding Personal achievement	28
Spouse starts work	26
Start or Finishing school	26

Change in living conditions	25
Revision of personal habits	24
Trouble with Boss	23
Change in work hours, conditions	20
Change in residence	20
Change in schools	20
Change in recreational habits	19
Change in social activities	18
Mortgage or loan under $10,000	18
Easter season	17
Change in sleeping habits	16
Change in number of family gatherings	15
Vacation	13
Christmas season	12
Minor violation of law	11

Arn, win, Ibid

While this is a relatively long list of typical events, it is by no means complete. For example it does not list the birth of a child. It does not mention major national tragedies, such as 9-11 and its impact on the U.S. population. This list of possibilities is as long as the list of different people and their uniqueness.

Often the only way to reach an extended family member or someone in your sphere of influence who is not presently open to the Christian faith is by being alert to periods of transition, during which time their receptivity may increase.

If we have been faithfully modeling the gospel, showing unconditional love, becoming a credible witness to God's grace in our own lives, faithful in prayer, it may be during one of these times that we will have the joy of seeing them respond to Christ's love.

Antithesis: If life is in a good / stable pattern it will be more difficult to break in with the Gospel. <u>They do not see the need.</u>

Second, Identify Homogeneous Groups

Society is made up of groups that stick together.

Each group acts as a barrier to the gospel.

The tighter the bonds, the more exclusive the group, the more it may act as a barrier.

However, when someone from that group becomes a Christ follower, everyone in that group may become more open and responsive, particularly if the new Christ follower is credible. If a movement starts, often almost entire groups come to Christ within a short period of time.

People will always be more responsive to someone else from their own homogeneous group.

Most people will be part of several homogeneous groups.

Family,
>   Work associates,
>>   Ethnic groups
>>   Social class
>>   Economic Class
>>   Neighborhoods (Closed neighborhoods)
>>   Academic groups
>>   Private clubs
>>   Clubs in general

If you are, or become, part of a homogeneous group you will have more influence within that group. Some groups will never accept anyone from outside, but new groups are forming every day. There are often groups that we naturally can become a part of, and with time can be become an insider within the group. This can be true, whether in a real functioning neighborhood association, a gardening club, or the local softball league.

Moving to a new community we have become part of a group of retirees that meet on a monthly basis. After a few years in this group we can begin to relate to people that we would otherwise have no connection to or influence. On occasion we have invited some of these persons to our home, this broadens our understanding and has given opportunity to listen.

Third, Give attention to Cycles of Responsiveness

Cycles of responsiveness may relate to transition times, but they don't necessarily.

Children will normally go through cycles when they are responsive.

Potential times:

> Age of beginning awareness
> Puberty
> Facing independence

Adults

Pay particular attention to the various rites of passage in which a person may be reevaluating their priorities.

Hiram

I first met Hiram when he and I were both contractors, subcontracting on the remodel of a large office building. Hiram was handling electrical changes. I was doing major demolition and new framing. Over time we became better acquainted as he and I from time to time would sub on other jobs at the same time. Eventually trust was established where I would often hire him as a sub on my own jobs.

Hiram was a rough and tumble sort of guy basically moral, but certainly didn't fit anywhere near church. If I was working as a sub on someone else's job, I normally largely disregarded the language and behavior of anyone that was not part of my own crew. If people were part of my crew, or working on my job, I was a little more involved, though still ignoring most language. The exception generally would have been if they started using Christ name in vain. Then I normally would have said something like, "would you please not say that, you are talking about my friend". I expect that was one of my first encounters with Mike related to spiritual things. Generally most guys respected that approach and except for times when they forgot, that would be the end of it.

At an earlier time, Hiram had been in a very serious accident. This was followed by many months in the hospital, pins and plates throughout his body to hold him together, and a lot of pain. Hiram became addicted to morphine. He eased himself off this addiction by becoming addicted to alcohol. So when I met him and got to know him well enough for him to talk about himself he referred to himself as a working alcoholic. Years went by, along with many conversations about spiritual things, some very brief, some longer conversations. Sometimes we would see each other on a daily basis. Sometimes months would go by without contact.

Months had gone by when I got a phone call from someone else in the construction industry who said, "Did you know that Hiram's son died?" I indicated that I had not known and they informed me that it was the result of an over dose. The death had taken place two days prior.

I immediately drove across town to their home. I found them in the kitchen. His wife's first words when I walked in the door were something like "would you do it". In my confusion I stammered out "do what". I soon discovered that after two days they did not have anyone to do the funeral and not knowing any active ministers wanted me to have their son's funeral service.

I determined that the least I could do was to make sure that Hiram, his family and friends knew where the source for hope in eternity lay. During that funeral, service I did my best to communicate that hope.

More years went by, during which time, Hiram being a very "good guy" built up an, "I owe you," record with me. Finally when Hiram was building an addition, on to his house and needed help making a difficult roof connection, he called me, and I finally had the opportunity, to give the assistance he needed, and pay up. Over the course of a couple of day we had more conversation, during which time Hiram told me that he had prayed to receive Christ, was reading his bible and spending time in prayer every day. He indicated that he had quit smoking, cut down significantly on his alcohol and thought with time he could cut it out completely. He said that his wife had started attending a local church, that if that worked out, (i.e. she felt accepted etc.) that he, himself, would then try to attend. Hiram has some very negative attitudes toward church stemming from being looked down on as the poor kid who was attending a more well to do church. These kinds of hurts make it even more difficult to find a church home, a process that is often difficult even for mature Christians.

Over time Hiram did begin to attend. I continued to pray for Hiram, and stop by as I had opportunity when back in the area. When I stopped by recently, his granddaughter whom they raised following her father's death, told me that Hiram was back in the hospital with a relapse of cancer. I visited him in the hospital, and we talked of his struggles and of our faith in God. A couple of weeks later his wife called to tell me Hiram had died. I look forward to seeing him when the Lord takes me home

Discussion Questions

Why is it important to look for responsive people?

How does Jesus discover responsiveness in the woman at the well?

What does Jesus consistently do to test responsiveness in the people with whom he talked?

In the story of the woman at the well described in John 4:7-42, where all did Jesus find responsive people? Where did he find homogeneous groups?

In John 4:35-38 what does Jesus teach his disciples about responsiveness?

In the story of my interaction with Hiram, do you believe that a positive result depended on the fact that I was a former pastor and could have the funeral service, or could anyone have had a similar impact?

What is the role of the church in ministering to a person and family such as this?

Prayer for real People, Realizing God's presence, power, leadership

What follows is a distillation. It is an attempt to summarize the basic principles of prayer. It results from the outlines of numerous sermons on prayer. In preparation for these messages I had read 15-20 books on prayer, and searched the Scriptures diligently. So! Take your time. Read each statement carefully. Think and do some of your own research in the Word. Learn how to pray for those around you who do not yet know Jesus.

Use of the phrase prayer for real people is very intentional. Most of the prayers that I hear are for the peace, prosperity, and especially for the health of people we know. These are certainly appropriate areas of prayer, and in some circumstances, God may want to answer to in the manner we desire. However, I suspect that God often has a different view of these issues than we do. He in fact may have allowed the very circumstance because he is attempting to bring focus on important issues that are being ignored or covered over.

Our first and most important issue in prayer is to know God. When we truly seek Him first, we place ourselves in a position where he can add the other things we need as well. When we seek first comfort, health, security for ourselves and others we are short sighted and may limit God.

Importantly I believe we usually then neglect the prayers that wrestle with the needs of the lost individuals that are all around. Praying for these individual takes our focus off ourselves, to something at the heart of God. We are changed in the process. We begin to see as he sees. We begin to love as he loves.

I remember, my prayer life as I have reflected on the needs being shared as I have listened to the Hiram's, Joes, Sheri's, Jill's, Cliffs, and Harold's. As I have listened to hopes and dreams, to marital discord, hopelessness, addiction, as people have begun to open themselves, or close themselves; it changes the way I pray.

I am then praying for real people and as God grips my heart I begin to pray for things that I know what God's will is and thus can pray with confidence. I know that God is there, and I know a closeness that does not happen when praying under any other circumstance. God has help me as I have prayed for other. He has helped me to see his heart

1. **Why does God want us to pray?**

    A. God wants us to develop our <u>character</u> through <u>prayer</u>

    God intends to <u>reveal</u> Himself to man. If you pray <u>little</u> you will know <u>little</u> about <u>God</u>

    B. Through prayer God intends to reveal His Purpose on earth and in our lives.
        If we don't <u>regularly</u> pray we will not know <u>God's will</u>.

    If we don't <u>pray</u> God will not <u>act</u>.

    If we don't <u>pray</u> we will lose our ability to <u>see God</u> clearly.

2. **Why don't we pray?**

    A. We don't pray because of weakness of the <u>body.</u>
    B. We don't pray because of the enmity of the <u>flesh.</u>
        Real prayer is <u>hard work</u> and runs counter to the desires of the flesh for <u>comfort, and pleasure.</u>

    We want to be and feel <u>self-sufficient</u>, and thus feel there is no <u>deep</u> <u>need</u> to pray.

C. We don't pray because of the <u>resistance</u> of the <u>enemy</u>. Since <u>prayer</u> is our most <u>important</u> weapon against <u>Satan</u>, this will be a primary place of attack.

3. **Climbing the Spiral Stairway ----- How to Pray**

Prayer is <u>conversation</u> between two people, <u>God</u> and <u>Me</u>. Mature prayer will include the following:

A. <u>Reading</u> God's Word expectantly. Reading God's word is part of Listening to God. His Spirit wrote it as he guided men. His Spirit will speak to us through it as we read and listen. Prayer then can then become an intelligent conversation.

B. <u>Meditation</u> on God's Word. As you "pray without ceasing" consistently repeat (chew on) the Word until it saturates your <u>mind.</u> This is God's Word. He can and will speak through it.

C. <u>Talking</u> specifically to God by giving thanks, expressing our adoration, confessing our sin, bringing our petitions and making <u>intercession</u> for others.

D. <u>Listen</u> until <u>light</u> begins to dawn on us and we have a new <u>vision</u> of <u>God.</u>

E. — <u>Acting</u> __ according to the love and greatness of God with <u>loving</u> <u>action</u> toward our fellow creatures.

The <u>Cycle</u> continues.

4. **How to fight against prayerlessness.**

There are twin evils that keep us from prayer:

A. There is the evil of <u>unwillingness</u> to pray.
B. There is the evil of <u>inability</u> to pray.

The Cure..........

Recognize …that we can't pray in our own <u>strength</u>, and instead <u>fight</u> the good fight of <u>faith</u> and seek and rely on the grace of God in our life.

Accept the fact that God will freely give us grace and <u>enable</u> us to pray.

We must begin to use God's <u>grace</u> to do the works he has prepared us to do, including the <u>work</u> of a personal, individual prayer life.

Make sure that we are acting in obedience to what God is showing us. There is no quicker way to kill the desire to pray than disobedience.

Getting truly involved in the lives of unbelievers around me, seeing their struggles, their needs, wrestling with their questions, I have found personally to be the quickest and easiest way to see not only my need to pray, but to be motivated to Pray. Loving involvement with others reveals both my weakness and need as well as theirs, thus a felt need to pray.

5. Conditions of the Unconditional promise. John 15:1-17
God will answer our prayer if.................

    A. We are <u>abiding</u> or remaining in Him
        How many times are the words abiding in Him or remaining in Him used in this passage?

    B. God's word <u>remains</u> in us.
        Often the real reason for our <u>unanswered</u> prayer stems from <u>failure</u> to abide in Him, or his word not abiding in us. Much of our praying is then self-centered, and inconsistent with God's purpose in our lives. The result is feebleness in our own <u>spiritual</u> life, and <u>feebleness</u> in our <u>prayers.</u>

In His <u>Word</u>, His will is <u>revealed</u>. As the <u>Word</u> abides in me, He <u>rules</u> me. My will becomes the empty <u>vessel</u> which His <u>will</u> fills; the <u>willing</u> instrument which His <u>will</u> wields. He fills my <u>inner being</u>.

6. Laws Governing Prayer

Natural laws are <u>real</u> and binding, and make physical life predictable.

Spiritual laws are <u>real</u> and <u>binding</u> and make spiritual life predictable.

What are the spiritual laws relating to prayer?

A. <u>Everything</u> must be done to the <u>glory</u> of God.
This is not just selfishness on God's part. It acknowledges who God in fact is. Acknowledgement of this is an element of our faith. Further, unbelievers will not come to trust God unless they see him as He is, in all His glory.

B. We must <u>pray</u> in the <u>name</u> of Jesus Christ.
This does not mean we are constantly repeating his name; rather it is an understanding that <u>everything</u> we are, and everything we have is a <u>gift</u> from God through Jesus Christ, and totally dependent on Him. Our prayer must acknowledge this and actively seek his glory.

C. We must <u>pray</u> according to the <u>will</u> of God.
D. We must <u>pray</u> with intense <u>desire.</u>
E. We must <u>ask</u> to <u>receive</u>.
<u>Asking</u> forces us to articulate our problem, therein God may lead us to find an answer. It also forces us to <u>admit</u> our needs, admit that we have come to the end of our own <u>resources</u>.

F. We must <u>ask</u> in <u>faith.</u>
G. We must <u>act</u> appropriately to our <u>faith.</u>

7. **How is God's will revealed to us through praying?**

   A. God's will is revealed through <u>creation</u>.

       Prayer cannot set aside spiritual law or physical law.

       It must work in harmony with God's will.

   B. God's will is revealed through <u>conscience</u>. However conscience must be thoroughly informed by God's written word, the bible.

   C. God's will is revealed through <u>Providence</u>. As God allows <u>open</u> and <u>closed</u> doors, we need to look carefully to see what God may be telling us.

   D. God's will is especially revealed through God' <u>Word</u>.

   E. To discover God's will in the bible, we must

       i.   <u>Study</u> the Bible as a <u>whole</u>
       ii. Practice <u>obedience</u> to the general will of God.
       iii. Ask God for <u>specific</u> direction as you <u>read</u> His word.
       iv. Be <u>Patient</u>.

8. **Praying according to God's will.**

   To pray according to God's will, the following must be true:

   A. My manner of asking is <u>according</u> to His <u>will</u>.
   B. The <u>thing</u> asked is according to His will.

   Barriers to knowing God's will:

       i.   Unwillingness to <u>obey</u> in areas we already know God's will.

ii.   Inaccurate <u>preconceptions</u>. I.e. of the nature of God, of what his will could be etc.

We should pray with boldness, because:
1.   God <u>wants</u> to reveal His will.
2.   His will is primarily known by <u>abiding</u>.
3.   God's will is usually <u>progressively</u> known.
4.   God's <u>will</u>, will not be accomplish unless we <u>pray</u>.

9.   The Ministry of Intercession

Intercessory Prayer is taking the time to let God help you begin to see your (friends) as God wants them to become (in all their potential – healed in their spirit, memories, emotions, and physical needs) and petition God to make it so.

A.   Men <u>confess</u> their sins and ask for forgiveness because they love <u>themselves</u>
B.   Men <u>petition</u> God to supply their needs because they love <u>themselves.</u>
C.   Men adore, worship, praise, and give thanks to God because they love <u>God</u>.
D.   Men engage in <u>intercessory</u> prayer because they love <u>others</u>, as well as God.
Love must be the motive for intercessory prayer. Intercessory prayer is the <u>main work</u> we can do in ministry to others. It is tough, hard <u>work</u>. It is taxing <u>labor</u>. It is <u>wrestling</u> before God.

Intercessory prayer is not generally the first thing we do in prayer. Thanksgiving, confession, surrender, just listening to God, those things that insure I am staying "in Christ" are essential. However, frankly, if you are not taking time to intercede for a person, (talking to God in behalf of an individual) you have absolutely no business talking to them about God, for it indicates that you don't love them much and misunderstand your role. You are in danger of only being "a resounding gong or a clanging cymbal."

10. The scriptural basis for Intercession.
Intercession is essentially the priestly role. See I Peter 2:4-10

1. The work of the <u>priest</u> is to represent God to the people, and the people to God.
2. The priest must be <u>holy</u>. Remember we are kept pure by walking in the light.
3. We are <u>priests</u> to each other by right of the new birth through Jesus Christ who is our High priest.

11. The Cure for Unbelief.
Our trouble with faith is a problem of <u>spiritual</u> eye sight.

We do not see things from God's perspective.

Spiritual Laws are interrelated.

Faith comes from hearing and understanding the Word.

We must <u>believe</u> God to pray.

We must <u>pray</u> to believe God.

We must <u>read</u> the word to know how to pray.

We must <u>pray</u> to understand the Word.

Faith is <u>decreased</u> in direct proportion to the concentration of my attention on physical realities to the <u>exclusion</u> of the <u>spiritual</u>.

Faith is <u>increased</u> as I continually read the word, spend time in prayer, and focus my attention on <u>spiritual</u> realities.

12. Apply prayer principles to interacting with unbelievers

Prayers God wants to say yes to

God wants all men to be saved; however, God does not answer prayer in a vacuum. He operates within a set of boundaries, boundaries that relate to his nature as a loving, holy, almighty God. These boundaries include praying according to His will.

These boundaries also relate to prayers that do not violate the will of the persons involved in our prayers. God will work patiently, he may allow or bring trouble, he will speak to us through guilt, dis-ease, loneliness, lack of purpose, beauty, design, other people, insight, fulfillment, thankfulness, birth of a child, responsibility, but while God is patient, He will never force a person to choose Himself.

So, we need to thoughtfully consider how we pray. We need to talk together in our small groups, seeking to know God's purpose, praying accordingly, with agreement together as we pray.

Discussion Questions

1. What is the time relationship in your prayer life between prayers of petition, praise, adoration, and intercession? What do you think it should be?
2. What would help you in your prayer life for others?
3. When trying to discern whether to talk with a friend, or what issues to discuss, how important is Spirit lead promptings?
4. How do we tell the difference between Spirit lead promptings and our own impressions and attempts at "good deeds"?
5. How often to do you discover opportunity to show love or speak the words of the gospel, when you have not been specifically praying? How often does opportunity come if you have been specifically and deliberately praying for unsaved persons?
6. Do you ever pray specifically that God would open your eyes to the felt needs around you?
7. What are some of the specific prayers we might pray, that we already know are within God's will?
8. We know that God "is not willing that any should perish, but that all might come to repentance." How does this influence the way we pray?

Assignment

1. Fill out the Web of Relationship form as completely as possible
2. Fill out an Extended Family Member Personal Profile on at least one person in your web of relationships.
3. Fill out your Disciple making plan for the person you profiled.
4. Have this information with you for our discussions during next week's session on Webs of Relationship, and the followings weeks planting and cultivating the seed.
5. We will also want to pray specifically with you, for both you and your friend during and after this time together.

Webs of Relationship

God has uniquely placed you where you are. You are a part of a family. You have a unique personality, unique gifts, and abilities. No one else in this world has or will have the exact sphere of influence, or influence within that sphere that you do.

In some instances you may be the only person, through whom Christ may touch a person whom you touch with your life. You may be the only person with the unique personality, the right gifts, the right manner of expressing love, the right manner of expressing your faith, the right timing; to touch persons in your sphere of influence. In some instances your introduction of these persons to the pastor or someone else in the church may be the exact thing that God can use. In other instances the Pastor or some other religious person would be the worst possible person in contact with your friend. You alone may be uniquely suited to relate the good news at this specific time and place in their life.

God has gifted some as Evangelists. These individual are unique and often use their gifts in such a way as to bring many to Christ through preaching and other methods that appeal to large groups. However, God has called all of his followers to proclaim the good news. While some gifts are uniquely suited to other ministries and many are rightfully so using them in these ways, the absence of the gift of evangelism may make you the perfect person to relate the gospel through your lifestyle to some of those whom God has placed around you. If you're a follower of Christ, then you are called, equipped, and expected to share the gospel using the unique abilities and personality God has given you.

Church historian Scott Latourette has observed that," the primary change agents in the spread of faith......were the men and women who earned their livelihood in some purely secular manner, and spoke of their faith to those whom they met in the natural fashion." Latourette, a History of the Expansion of Christianity. Volume I, P. 116

"Webs of common kinship (the larger family), common friendships (friends and neighbors) and common associates, (special interests, work relationships, and recreation) are still the paths most people follow in becoming Christians today." Arn, How Disciples are Made. P. 43

Win and Charles Arn give seven reasons that Oikos or household relationships are effective in spreading the good news of Jesus Christ.

1. These relationships provide a natural network for sharing the good news of God's redemptive love.
2. Because of an existing trust relationship these persons tend to be receptive.
3. These relationships allow for unhurried and natural sharing of God's love.
4. These relationships provide natural support when the web member comes to Christ.
5. These relationships result in the effective assimilation of new converts into the church.
6. These relationships tend to win Entire Families.
7. These relationships provide a constantly enlarging source of new contacts.

Bill Hybels in His book Walk Across the Room highlights the fact that in the average church, "the longer a person attends church, the fewer evangelistic discussions they engage in with family members and friends. The fewer presentations of the life-changing plan of salvation are given, and the fewer invitations to events that attractively present the message of Christ." Hybels, Bill, <u>Just Walk Across the Room</u>, Grand Rapids, MI: Zondervan, 2006

This is true because <u>the longer it has been since the Christ-follower began his journey, the</u> <u>fewer the number of friends outside the faith</u>.

If you do not have any non-Christian friends, it is time that you walk across the room and start making some.

If you do not have any non-Christian friends you need to seriously pray about whether God would have you become involved in community organizations where you can and will meet unbelievers.

Perhaps you should volunteer for an organization meeting needs of children, elderly, etc. using the gifts that God has given you.

<u>Identification and next step process</u> for discovering those to whom God may want you to minister.

Step Number one.

If you have some non-Christian friends, begin listing them as completely as possible on your Web of Relationships work sheet. See Appendix.

If you have no, or very few, non-Christian friends, begin listing those persons that you encounter in your daily activities with whom there is some possibility of getting acquainted and forming a friendship. Don't know their name? Describe them and where you would expect to encounter them again. Determine to introduce yourself and get at least a first name. If you make a long enough list, there will be someone who would at least be glad to know that someone was praying for them. If the list of potential unbelievers with whom you might become friends is still very short, consider local community organizations that you could become active in, wherein you might make friends and perhaps also have a positive influence.

Step Number two.

Enter the name of a person from your list on the personal profile sheet. Begin to fill out the sheet. If you don't yet know the information, make a note to yourself to discover this information, as you practice the habit of listening.

Step Number three.

Enter the name from you profile sheet on your disciple-making plan sheet.

Prayerfully consider the information you have and determine your next steps.

Example:

Planting and cultivating the Seed

To this point I have downplayed our use of words, because we are so prone to speak when speech is inappropriate, however, give the right time and place words are absolutely essential, so let's talk about the process.

Sharing the Gospel in bits and pieces

People do not come to Christ, in an intellectual vacuum.

It is not enough to model the gospel of Christ if people have no idea of who Christ is, what his life and death were all about, or what he can do for them.

<u>Words are important.</u>

God the **<u>Word</u>** was with God in the beginning, (John 1:2) He became <u>flesh</u> and dwelt among us. (V.14) God Spoke to us through the prophets "at many times and various ways, but in these last days he has spoken to us by his Son." Hebrews 1:1-2

The words of Christ followers continue to be important, because God rarely if ever speaks to people in a vacuum. He uses words and experiences to build on one another to bring insight and meaning, which allows first the germ and then the full flowering of Faith.

However, even if we have been a faithful model of the life of Christ that is within, even if we have faithfully been listening and discovering another person's story, even if we have perceived their felt needs and have become aware of responsiveness on their part, <u>rarely will we have the opportunity to share our story and Christ story in full at one sitting.</u>

Normally a large portion of our story and of His story is shared in bits and pieces over an extended period of time.

A few years ago I was working at one of our construction sites, when I spotted my wife walk down the sidewalk past one of the windows. I immediately responded by saying "Man, you should have seen that beautiful woman who just walked past". One of my workers was very disappointed that he had missed her. I responded, "I am not about to miss her!" and headed for the door, with my worker right at my heels. Imagine his embarrassment when he met my wife at the door!

Having fun at someone else's expense? Maybe, but also having an awareness of where many of my workers were coming from, demonstrating that I also am alive, and making myself open to further discussion which came a few days later, with questions about how I, a Christian, handles his sexuality.

This discussion started with their perception of how I was, and how I behaved. In summary, I responded by letting them know that that I was no different than they were except for presence of Christ within and the changes that he was making.

Secrets that should not be kept Secret.

The words of the Gospel can easily be shared if we keep in mind a few key secrets. We need to plant seed thoughts at appropriate times.

Seed thoughts are thoughts that are not necessarily obvious for what they are, but over time can begin to grow as the person remembers and considers the implications.

My worker had to consider the possibility that I as a Christian might have answers that not only could be attractive but solve problems that he and others he knew were facing.

Seed thoughts can be planted related to every conceivable area of human need and Christ's ability to relate to the need.

Christ's parables are examples of seed thoughts. None of them tells the complete gospel story in one setting, yet taken together we begin to get the picture.

The possibility for seed thoughts is as unlimited as the fullness of God's word and the Holy Spirits ability to access our minds and bring them to our attention.

Nicholas Sparks whose faith had matured and solidified, in his book <u>Three Weeks with My Brother,</u> Readers Digest Condensed books, Vol. 1, 2005 speaks of a conversation with his brother whose faith had floundered. The conversation took place toward the end of a 3 week round-the-world trip. Prior to the trip they had lost their mother at age 47 after a fall from a horse, followed by the loss of their father in an auto accident about 7 years later, and their younger sister within another two years resulting from a brain tumor.

"Why do I get the impression that you think the solution to all my problems is to be more like you?"

"Hey, if the shoe fits…" He shrugged, and I laughed.

"So you still think you have to take care of me, huh?"

"Only when I think you need it, little brother."

"And what if I started talking to you about God, because I think you need it?"

"Go ahead," he said. "I'll listen."

Above me, the sky was filled with stars, and the words rose up almost unexpectedly: *"God keeps his promise, and He will not allow you to be tested beyond your power to remain firm; at the same time you are put to the test, He will give you the strength to endure it, and so provide you with a way out."*

Micah glanced over at me. Despite the darkness, I could see him raise his eyebrows.

"First Corinthians," I said. "Chapter Ten."

"Impressive."

I shrugged. "I just always liked that verse. It reminds me of the footprints story….you know, the one where God walks with a man on the beach. Scenes from the man's life flash in the sky, and during flashbacks of the most trying times of the man's life, he sees only one set of foot prints. Not because God abandoned the man in times of need, but because God carried the man."

Micah was quiet for a moment. "So you don't think he abandoned us?"

"No. And I don't think he wants you to abandon him either."
Sparks, Nicholas, <u>Three Weeks with My Brother</u>, Readers Digest Condensed books, Vol. 1, 2005

This incident not only illustrates planting seed thoughts at appropriate times, but it also illustrates excellent use of Scripture, mixed with bits and pieces of our own story.

When we fully dwell in Christ, not just an occasional visit, saturate ourselves with His word, not only will the Holy Spirit bring appropriate

Scripture to mind, at the right time, he can and will let us know what and when to share our own thoughts and experience.

We need to practice the "With me" principle.

Alice and Sherry moved into the same community at about the same time. Their spouses had similar employment. The nature of their work brought the couples together and Alice and Sherry became good friends. With many shared interests they spend considerable time together.

As time went on Sherry began to get acquainted with people in her new church home. She increasingly got involved with church activities and with these new friends to the point that she was turning down most of Alice's invitations. There came a point when Alice became offended, and made not only a conscious decision to stop asking, but took a negative attitude toward Sherry.

A mutual acquaintance heard comments from both Alice and Sherry. While

Sherry in reality actually did really like Alice as a friend, and was concerned about Alice's relationship with God, she did not understand the "with me" principle, and allowed as she put it "life to get in the way". She failed to understand the importance of being a friend, to set priorities, and perhaps missed God's will for her at that moment.

While Church relationships are important and should be treated as such, those who take seriously the role God wants them to play in their sphere of influence, must also pray and fully consider the question. Who are those person around me with whom God want me to continue developing a lasting relationship?

We may legitimately not have time, we may have a multitude of other lacks, but the more that we are able to include our unbelieving friends with other positive Christians that we know, the more likely it will be that one or more of them will be able to relate to this person, and that they will be drawn to Christ through seeing Christ in his followers. Perhaps the biggest mistake sherry made in the incident just related, was that she did not find a way to include Alice with some of her new Christian friends and their activities that were not threatening.

Do you have activities outside the church with your Christian friends, could you include a non-Christian friend as well?

We need to introduce them to other positive Christians.

This concept will be discussed more fully in the session on the place of the Church in presenting an accurate picture of Christ.

Developing your stories

In the next session we will be spending time trying to get the essence of your story into a short, clear, presentation that you will be able to use effectively as the times arise in the future.

Here we want to look at snap shots of your life that illustrate what God has done to change you as you have confronted the ongoing challenges of life. These are parts of your total story, but often can be related quickly in bits and pieces without being threatening to your friend.

What are some of the unique ways that God has impacted your life? Please make as complete a list as possible.

With each of these facets of your life, what was your life like before Christ, how is it different now?

In circumstances that have occurred since faith in Christ, how has your faith impacted your life? How, is your life different than it would have been before Christ, how is it different than what you typically see around you?

What about the areas, in which you still struggle, the areas in which you suffer defeat, how does Christ fit into your life in these situations?

What have you learned through disappointment, through times in which it seems like God is not there?

Articulating the Gospel

Words must start where people are

When Jesus spoke to the woman at the well, he spoke first of living water. He progressed from there, both by giving the woman information that made her curious, followed by responding to her questions. When Jesus invited James,

John, Peter, and Andrew there is evidence of an ongoing prior relationship. He approached them with an invitation to a higher purpose; come follow me and I will make you fishers of men, i.e., in contrast with fishing for fish. In His conversation with Nicodemus, a teacher of Israel, Jesus spoke of the birth of the spirit, of a relationship resulting from faith in God's Son. When Jesus articulated the words of the gospel, he always started from where they were already at in their lives. He proceeded from there in a manner that aligned with something they could understand.

Understanding Jesus approach underscores the importance of really listening to people until we have a clear understanding of where they are at in their attitude, and in their understanding of the gospel. Listening will enable us to have a clearer picture of their needs and what they might understand and respond to.

Understanding Jesus approach also underscores the importance of a clear knowledge of the word, such that you can share relevant aspects of the gospel with individuals as their felt need requires. The gospel is multifaceted. We all start with a tiny picture that expands as we gain information. We never understand the whole in this life. Individuals come to Christ at many points along the way. As we dwell in Christ, as we experience Him in our lives through His word, prayer, obedience, and fellowship with other believers, we will come to an increasing understanding of the whole gospel and can share what is needed with a person with whom we have become comfortable, and who has become comfortable with us. It is at this point that we can have assurance that God's Spirit will guide us and give us insight and the words that we should speak.

Connie was a young woman in her mid-twenties. We had known her over a 3 year period, with significant interaction on a weekly basis. She had sought us for counsel numerous times related to her personal life as well as related to some of our shared activities. She had a ritualistic Christian background with no clear understanding. She had shown openness to church involvement, but always was too busy and had no felt need that made attending a priority. She had many tangled relationships. These relationships created felt need – for something. (Most people don't know what they need, they just know they need.) She had attend Church with us a couple of time, and suggested attending again, however I knew that attending without more basic information, could confuse rather than help, that a couple of exposures to information and activity that did not relate to her needs could push her away rather than draw her to Christ. I did not want her there until she would have a reason to stay, along with a group of persons who would help her along the way.

We had shared our lives and meals with her many times. We knew and she knew that we were moving out of the area. She requested to take us out for a meal. During this meal I ask if we could set down together in the privacy of our home and I could share with her background information about a relationship with Christ that would make Church meaningful. She was eager so we set a time.

Because of her low information level I believed it was important that I give a clear overall view. I simply started at the beginning and began to give a brief survey of the history of God and man. We traced through creation, sin, Abraham, God's promises, Israel's sin and failure, the promised redeemer, and God becoming a man in Jesus Christ. When I said God became a man in Jesus, she look at me and said; "I did not know that". We continued and I shared the basics of a relationship with God. As I turned to discover whether she wanted this kind of relationship, ready to explain that I did not want to force her into something she was not ready for, she looked at my wife and I with tear in her eyes and a eager yes, virtually before I could ask. Following prayer she responded, man I have got goose bumps.

Now she was ready and eager for Church. Now our responsibility of discipling was just beginning. It was here at this level that the importance of small groups and large groups; the fellowship of the Church was just beginning.

In writing this I am including resources related to various facets of the gospel; however every person and every situation is unique. You are a unique person, God will use you uniquely. **You really do need to take time to prepare yourself.**

This preparation should be a part of your dwelling in Christ and his Word. Prepare to use His Word through the leadership of His Spirit to share with those God has given you in God's time and place.

Words must center on Jesus Christ Himself.

Speaking of God's claims are irrelevant until......

Until a person really comprehends who Jesus Christ is, His credibility as God, his credibility as a God that truly does love them personally. Until a person understands Jesus as offering life itself, as one who ultimately destroys pain, suffering and evil, until then **His claims are irrelevant.** Thus when sharing the gospel with another person we do not start with His claims on their lives.

We start with who Jesus is.

As in the Gospel of John, we share Him as the "light of the world", as the "water of life", as the "good shepherd", as the "resurrection and the life", as the "way, the truth, and the life". **We help people to discover Jesus as God become man, through whom we can come to know God Himself.**

Knowing God is our ultimate goal.

Only when people come to really understand who Jesus **is**, are they in any position to truly consider what their response to him should be. Until this time there is nothing to inspire faith, there is nothing to command respect, there is nothing to produce hope, and there is certainly nothing to overcome their fear, or rebellion against God Himself.

We automatically assume that those with some exposure to the church would know who Jesus is. However this is not necessarily true. In fact the opposite may be true. For many the exposure to God through Jesus Christ, at best has been superficial. There has been little or no exposure to persons or congregations, of vital faith. There has never been and real exposure to the Word of God itself.

If they heard preaching at all, it often majored on minor or periphery issues. It may have emphasized social moral issues, often telling what we should do and be, without ever really connecting this with the life giving power of Jesus Christ who is the only one to ever truly empower rightness in our life. Add to this the confusion hypocrisy and other deadly issues in the church itself and many never comprehend even superficially who Jesus really is.

Words must share essential Gospel elements

When I begin to share the words of the gospel with a person whom I have discovered is confused by the different emphasis of different Churches, I usually start by explaining that while there are many areas of disagreement and different emphasis; that among churches who accept the bible as the authoritative word of God there is total agreement regarding the core issues. I often go on to explain that the areas of disagreement center around life and practice, rather than on the core issues of salvation itself. I assure them that they can sort those issues out later, as they get into the word, and begin to experience God in their own life. In other words I attempt to help them see not only the diversity within the church, but also its essential unity.

What then are the absolute core issues?

1. Man has become separated from God through sin as a result of his own unbelief and disobedience.

2. Sin has brought about spiritual death. Aside from a remedy, the final result of this spiritual death, is physical, and eternal death and separation from God.

3. There is nothing that man can do totally on his own to bring about Salvation.

4. Jesus Christ, born of the Virgin Mary, is God having become a man, fully God, fully man. Jesus is the exact representation of who God is. Jesus reveals God to Man

5. Jesus Christ was crucified on the Cross, died as an atonement for man, thus removing the barrier between God and man. He bodily rose from the dead again the third day, and is alive for evermore.

6. Salvation is the result of a choice of faith in God through Jesus and the unmerited Grace of God.

7. Salvation comes as a free gift of God to all those who fully place their faith in Jesus Christ as their savior.

8. It is through God's power received by faith that we are enabled live in relationship with God, and a life pleasing to Him. We cannot do it on our own.

9. The ultimate destination is to be brought back into fellowship with God Himself, our separation has ended. We are prepared to spend eternity with Him.

There are very large number of other doctrines which are essential to growth in the grace of God, some of these may be very helpful for an unbeliever to understand to assist them to place their faith in Jesus Christ, but I believe that we must be very careful that we do not place any burdens of over information on them that will hinder their movement toward God. Most of the time, simple is best.

If they are asking questions that relate to the essence of the Gospel; questions that are truly issues that they are struggling with, then we need to carefully answer those questions, or find someone else who can. However, if they are simply asking all kinds of questions that are simply a smoke screen to stay away from the issues of their own rebellion and unbelief, then we need to steer them back to the issues that are separating them from God, or wait until a time when they are in fact open to what God has to say in their life.

Possible approaches

When the time and the place is right to share the words of the Gospel there are many possible ways that this can be done. It is important that you do have some kind of clarity as you walk through this important time. It is important to remember that God's word emphasizes being prepared to give an answer to the hope that we have. You do not want to be a slothful servant. Without some kind of clarity, it is very easy to wander all over the map and never get where you want to go. Satan is a master not only of deceit, but also of confusion. This is an opportunity to assist your friend to focus on the truth; the truth about themselves, the truth about God, and the truth about the world in which they live.

If you are a mature Christian, very knowledgeable of the Word of God from your own immersion in it, with a good grasp of the basic issues of salvation, with an understanding of how the gospel relates to the various areas of human need; with the Holy Spirits assistance you probably do not need to follow a prepared plan. With enough experience of God and with sharing the word perhaps you should not, because with God's assistance, you can be speaking from the heart of God to their heart.

If you are a novice, a prepared plan, if not a must, it is still highly recommended. You can be very upfront. Let them know that you are new to this, but also let them know what God is doing and has already done in your life. This may be a time to share a good bit of your story as well as God's story. People get excited when they see the reality of experiencing God in someone else's life.

There are many plans available. I am not going to detail any of them here. You can seek them out and have them available in booklet form to carry with you.

A few memorized verses of Scripture can easily give you a brief outline. A single verse guideline can be found in Romans 6:23. "For the wages of Sin is death, but the gift **of God** is eternal life through Christ Jesus our Lord." I emphasized various words. By doing this in your mind as you share it with a person, you can easily share God's love. If a person is truly responsive to God, as you share aided by the Holy Spirit, it does not require much on your part except your love and availability.

Discussion Questions:

What facts about Christ does a person need learn in order to come to saving faith?

What is the least that a person can believe and be saved?

Section Four

The Christ follower's interaction with other believers in the process of making disciples

Introduction: problems and concerns

One of the primary points of this book is that **God has, and continues do his work with people, through people.** It is also true that this is generally accomplished in some manner through his Spirit. However the Spirit does not normally work independent of people, or without their willing and even eager participation. This is true of God's work in and through what we call the church.

So! If God wants to work through his Spirit in and through his people the Church; if God wants to minister to the church, and beyond the church to the world, what does this look like?

As stated at the beginning of the book: **the body of Christ, the Church is meant to interact**. We have looked at our interaction with God himself. We have looked at our interaction with unbelievers. We look now at our interaction with other believers, especially as it relates to seeing new people come to faith in Jesus Christ.

Until now we have focused primarily on our interaction as individuals. **We focus now on the "body" the Church, working together as a unit.** In the Church, while remaining individuals, we are also intimately connected as part of a body. We cannot remain healthy and effective as individuals "in Christ" without also having a healthy connection to and interaction within the Church. The Church itself cannot remain healthy without a healthy connection and interaction of individuals.

This interaction is at several levels. There are interactions for example between pastor and congregation. There are interactions of other leaders with other parishioners. There is interaction on the level of congregational assembly as a whole. There is interaction when gathered in small groups, whether for study, work or fellowship.

The manner in which each of these levels of interaction relate to Christ and to each other, are foundational, and critical to whether the local body of Christ, is accomplishing its intended ministry, to itself and the community within which God has placed it.

In the parable of the sower Jesus speaks of 4 types of soil; the pathway, rocky, weedy, and the good or cultivated soil. Each of us at some point in our lives have found ourselves properly described by each of the first three. Hopefully we strive to be the later type of soil.

In the course of this book, I have named a number of individuals with whom we have had contact, who have made the decision to believe and receive Jesus into their lives. I wish I could report that all of them have quickly found their way into the church, grew rapidly and were fruitful and flourishing in their faith.

Unfortunately, more often than not, that has not been true. In all instances we do have to consider the soil, and each person's choices. However, if we stop there, placing the full blame on each individual, we may ease our conscience, but fail to see the truth. **We also have to look at the Church, its life and vitality, its reception of people, its preparedness for birthing and nurture, and its ability to love in real meaningful ways.**

When I spoke of Eric, I indicated I was "back in an area". I was visiting relatives in an area in which, I had previously lived. I had moved. In other instances the persons who came to Christ moved. In virtually each situation in which a person's faith has floundered, someone moved and there was no assimilation into the Church.

Our friends Sheri and bill moved several times. In each instant they sought out a church, visiting more than one. This included both of them in spite of his not reaching a choice to believe. In each incident the church attended appeared to represent faith which was nominal and reduced to a ritual. Perhaps worst of all, no one reached out to them. At this point they are lost to the Church. In spite of this I see occasional evidence of faith and or seeking and openness.

About 10 years after they moved from our area, at their invitation we traveled to their home for a visit. We were included in a two night camping trip with three additional families. There we were encouraged to talk about our faith and share a devotional time. God is still working even where the church may be part of the hindrance. Pray with me for these families.

In spite of my background and openness to others, I found that it is very difficult to be really included in churches that I have attended. Most people while outwardly welcoming while at church, already have full lives. Beyond church services almost no one gives a thought to those not part of their circle. A often repeated scenario; those with weak or non-existent faith are lost to the church, perhaps to the kingdom. Because I have been persistent I have found ways to become a part. My heart cries for the day when, especially for new believers, there is an easy way in.

In this section we are looking at the ministry of the Church as it relates to itself in the total process of discipling. This relates to the unbeliever who is yet outside the Church, but it also relates to the new / and / or moving (I.E. new to our community or local church) believer. This is not just an academic study. This is real life and there are critical problems in the Church.

When viewing the local church we need to seek to understand all of the following factors:

The soil conditions represented by unbelievers,

The culture of our church,

The ease or difficulty of people actual becoming an insider in our fellowship,

And the spiritual life (soil condition) of those who are attending.

We need to be able to spot and include persons who stand at the door, ready to escape not because they are disinterested, but because they do not know the way in.

We need to see whether people are really connecting with others and growing in faith, or if they are just a familiar face, perhaps perceived as only a number.

We (someone, perhaps a small group leader) need to know them well enough to discern their needs and concerns. We thus can relate the Gospel to a person where they are at that point in time.

Ministries of the local church must keep each of these issues in clear focus if ministry is to be vital and life changing.

Primary areas of Group of Interaction

> Assembly for Celebration and Worship
> Assembly for study, fellowship, and prayer
> Assembly for group interaction in community ministry

Primary purpose of Assembly and Interaction

> Celebration and Worship
> Nurture and the discipling process
> Assimilation of new believers
> Assimilation of moving believers.
> Pastoral care for every one

The church assembled: reaching unbelievers

My circumstances in sharing the good news with others is not unusual in our society. People do move. Much of our society is very mobile. This cannot be avoided. It does however highlight our need to work together. It is a reminder that the stranger in our midst is always someone with needs. These needs cannot be met by any one other individual. It is a reminder that the church is not an individual. It is a multitude of individuals in groups large and small around the world.

Especially, the church is the local groups of Christ followers around me and the local church of which I am a part. I cannot flourish in my own relationship with Christ, let alone present Christ accurately and completely on my own. One individual acting alone cannot meet all the needs of another, especially the full range required to fully disciple others as mature Christ followers.

"Speaking the truth in love, we will in all things grow up into him who is the Head, that is, Christ. From him the whole body, joined and held together by every supporting ligament, grows and builds itself up in love, as each part does its work." Eph. 4:15-16

Our personal interaction with unbelievers to introduce them to Jesus Christ is one of the primary and natural results of all the interactions that are appropriate to a Christ follower. **This however is not a solo effort.**

You and I are each, only one member of the body of Christ. At our best, by ourselves we are a poor and very incomplete picture of what, and who, Christ is.

In contrast to our solo effort, when an unbeliever sees a group of vitally committed followers who are living together in harmony and love, each expressing themselves in the fullness of their own unique personality, and using the gifts God has uniquely given them; only then does the world around them, begin to see the fringes of who Christ really is.

Suppose that you were a specialist, if you were to dissect any body and study its individual cells, you might be able to identify the type of body it is taken from. Many could identify the type of body they were looking at if they looked at an organ of the body, or a part of the body such as a foot. The dumbest among us could identify a **whole body** with which they were familiar.

Unbeliever need to see the church as the body, functioning as a **healthy whole.** When this happens they begin to really understand who Christ is in His full glory. When they are touched by this fellowship and love they are drawn to Christ.

Interactive evangelism centers on individuals and their interactions, person to person, with those in their sphere of influence. Yet it falls far short if we attempt to do it by ourselves. We need the prayers and encouragement of others. We need their prayers, both for us and for those we touch. We need their ideas and input. Often we need their influence. Circles of influence often can and should merge.

For example, perhaps I am actively in touch with an unbeliever, I am praying, I am endeavoring to listen, to live a life of love. Perhaps this unbeliever is resistant to words. Perhaps they have been disillusioned by previous "church" contacts. I discover that another believer has contact through their children. That yet another has contact through work. We pray together, we arrange times of recreation together to begin to draw this individual into a circle of friendship and influence. I discover areas that are of concern to the unbeliever, areas that are or should be of concern to the church. Together we reach out to meet these needs.

Through listening to people, listening to God, we can discover possibilities that are endless. **This is not a solo effort.**

Even as Paul reminded the Corinthian's "The eye cannot say to the hand, 'I don't need you!'" We cannot say to the others in our church, "I do not need you".

Personally I have learned from experience that you cannot build a fire with one log. On many an occasion, when camping, I have wanted to conserve wood. I did not want it wet, so I simply rolled the wood apart. Individual logs always go out. Conversely, if the fire is burning down, and I want it hotter, I roll them together. Better yet add more wood to the fire.

Faith will be ignited, rekindled, encouraged as we of faith, share closely with one another in an atmosphere of love. Wholeness and healing, abundant living in Christ happens when, persons of faith commit to Christ, to each other, and to reaching the lost around them; encourage each other, teach each other, and become accountable to one another in the love of Christ.

Not only do we desperately need each other within the Church, but the unbeliever needs to see the bigger picture, to begin to see enough of who Christ is to place their faith in him. This becomes even more essential as they begin the discipling process, following their initial decision.

Assimilation and discipling of new people

The high level of importance for ongoing ministries that build and encourage people is noted when we read the words of John Wesley. "Follow the blow, never encourage the devil by snatching souls from him that you cannot nurture, - - - converts without nurture are like still-born babies." Outler, Albert. Evangelism in the Wesleyan Spirit, Evangelistic Work Publisher, Nashville, TN 1971, P. 23.

Yet, as important as the discipling process is, it cannot be done alone. This nurturing or discipling requires the active involvement of the church truly acting as Christ's body. It requires the church to work together within its community of fellowship. There must be gifted hands involved in service, teaching lips rendering wisdom through instruction. There must be daily words of wisdom and encouragement. It requires eyes of discernment, with constant expressions of love, grace and forgiveness.

Sometimes it requires words of correction and rebuke.

New Converts, and especially new individuals who are still uncertain about the Christian faith, cannot be simply left to themselves to fit into the worship services of the typical church. They cannot be left to sort things through on whatever preaching fare happens to be present at that moment. They cannot be left to attempt to make new friends, especially left to make new friends at a time when they may not even know their need for Christian fellowship. If they are left to do all this on their own, they are not likely to survive. These individuals need someone with eyes to see them, to come along side, to draw them into the larger fellowship of a group who will surround them with love.

Assume that you are a believer, that you are part of a vital, encouraging small group. As you listen and relate to a person in your circle of influence, you discover evidence that is God working in their life. You discover openness on their part. You begin to introduce that person to your core group of believers a little at a time, whether fun social occasions, a work project of mutual interest, or a serious bible study. At some point that individual comes to know Christ. They are then introduced fully to your small group, and then or prior they are introduced to the worshiping church as a whole. Now with support from the small group members, both the opportunity and the probability of them becoming a real disciple, has been immeasurable increased.

We may do a lot as individuals, but going it alone, not only is ineffective, it runs counter to the "body" principle. The body needs both bones, and skin. It needs hands and feet, eyes and ears.

The church Assembled: Working together in small groups

Small Groups: <u>The basic unit of the Church is the small group.</u>

From its infancy the small group has been at the heart of the church as evidenced in Acts 2:46 – 47; "They broke bread in their homes and ate together with glad and sincere hearts, praising God and enjoying the favor of all the people. And the Lord added to their number daily those that were being saved." This setting of small group function did not significantly change until the time of Constantine in the third century, when the church began to be institutionalized.

It was in the setting of small groups of people, in the midst of persecution and martyrdom, that the early church not only survived, it thrived. Some unbelieving historians, not understanding the Holy Spirit as the early churches source of life and power, even credit the intimacy and encouragement of the small group for the world changing influence of Christianity in the first three centuries.

Following are some principles and practices essential to small groups.

1. Follow the Master's Plan

The early church had the best example.

Small groups were Jesus Christ's plan for building disciples. Christ preached to the masses. He ministered to individuals, but he walked with people (his disciples) through the discipling process in a small group.

We see His focus on three; Peter, James, and John; the 12, the 70, and the expanding circle outward to the multitudes. His example shows us both the difficulty and the fruit of taking the time, and making the effort, to work with a small group.

Encouragement to develop small groups should not be taken to imply that they are fun and easy, rather they are encouraged knowing they are essential to the often costly work of making disciples.

When a couple does the usually pleasurable work of conceiving a child, they often forget, or are oblivious to the pain and pleasure that will later accompany child birth and child rearing. Yet, few are the parents that were they able to live life over, that would not have children.

Certainly, small groups can and will have difficulties, yet when people are truly seeking vital relationship with God, walking in obedience, God can and will use each difficulty to bring the group into a deeper relationship with Himself and with other believers.

If we look closely we will see that this benefits the leader of a small group, as well. Evidence shows that while Jesus was the son of God, he still wanted and needed fellowship. We as leaders need not only fellowship; we need the group to inspire our faith. We need the small group for accountability and to assist in our own discipling. Discipling others has without any doubt on my part, been the largest contributor to discipling me.

Back in the late 70's, Robert E. Coleman in His book <u>The Master Plan of Evangelism</u>, Old Tappan, NJ, Fleming H. Revell Co. 1963 probably was the first to introduce me to Jesus method of working with His disciples. Most disciples are slow to learn, I am embarrassed at how slow I often am. I am perhaps only now really beginning to fully grasp the implications and importance of really investing oneself in being discipled in a small group, and in turn, investing oneself to disciple others.

However, as Coleman clearly points out in his book, Jesus is not only to be our master, he is the master leader of a small group. His technique is perfect. His love is everlasting. His teaching never misses the mark. He is our mentor not just in life, but as we try to understand and grow through the small group. When we fail to follow His example, we do so to our own hurt, and to the hurt of the church. We do so to the hurt of the mission of discipling, that Christ wants to do through us.

In spite of some early awareness of the potential, and the need for discipling people through small groups, I never took the time for serious discipling in small groups. At the time I really did not know how. I did not really understand or believe in its importance or effectiveness. However, probably the biggest reason was because I was in too big a hurry. I wanted to see converts. How foolish! We never can bear fruit that lasts in our own strength. It happens only through the strength of His Spirit, as he walks in and through us, in His timing and His way.

The Church tends to make one of two errors. Either we focus on making converts who are never discipled, and often still born, or we focus on forever discipling without purpose; forever maturing people without daily involvement with others that is essential to any real depth of love and maturity.

Billy Graham ministered to millions with many conversions, but as he neared the end of his ministry, he is quoted as saying;" if I had it to do over I would spend more time discipling people." Unknown source

Throughout His ministry Jesus continued to preach to the masses, however this was not his primary focus. Jesus invested himself primarily in those chosen 12 who were known as apostles.

The difficulty of this ministry even for Jesus, is seen in the disciple's regular rivalry, their bad attitudes, their slowness and even failure to understand and grasp issues that may seem obvious to us. Jesus spent an intensive 3 years with the 12, yet to the end they were often indecisive and confused. Even Jesus, had a drop out, who betrayed him.

Prior to Pentecost and the out pouring of the Spirit, Christ's efforts looked like a failure. Just prior to the crucifixion, the disciples failed to understand some of the most basic of concepts. The success of Christ's investment in the 12, the 70, is seen following Pentecost.

These disciples were obedient to him. As promised by Christ, at Pentecost they were filled with the Holy Spirit. Following this they received continued power and instruction through Him. Then the disciples, in the words of their opponents "have turned the world upside down".

An important lesson should be noted here: **As important as the filling of the Holy Spirit is, <u>discipling is also needed</u>.**

In the example of Christ's work with the 12, much of the discipling process took place prior to the filling with the Holy Spirit. Most individuals don't even become aware of their own inner unsurrendered self until after conversion. Only then do they become aware of a divided self, a self that must be surrendered in order for Christ to be Lord, for the Holy Spirit to fully indwell the heart. For example would Peter have been prepare for Pentecost if Christ's had not allowed him to first deny him three times prior to His death on the cross.

God can do anything, but He generally does not work significantly through individuals who are unsurrendered, uneducated in the things of God. Learning the things of God, learning to surrender, are generally best learned through consistently walking with him along with other believers who are in close communion with God and fellowship with each other.

I speak of the kind of discipling that can only happen over time as we walk with people, we show them the way, encourage one another's faith, we pray together in faith and see God work. I speak of fellowship together as we pray and study, as we learn to trust one another, and share our needs; as we share our failures as well as our successes, as we serve together, as we witness together and yes as we have fun in recreation.

The obverse of this is that as important as the discipling process is: if it is done in the absence of the filling of the Holy Spirit in the lives of the disciples and the disciple, nothing will be accomplished.

We need to study carefully the example of Jesus in this discipling process. While on this earth, Jesus was with the disciples to disciple them. When He ascended, he indwelled them with His Spirit to not only be with them as previously, but now to be in them.

Later in life as I realized the importance of this small group discipling process, I began to create opportunities for myself. Until then, I had had very little opportunity for this kind of instruction, (discipling group) and encouragement to my Christian faith. I believe my progress and effectiveness suffered greatly as a result of this isolation. We need more than sermons including mine. We need more than university or seminary, we need more than the best of books, or even hours spent in the word by ourselves. <u>For our faith to flourish, we need the vital contact of person to person, in small groups within the body of Christ</u>. <u>Vital contact among persons who are determined to grow in their faith.</u> Within this context we also need to be active in ministry outside the body with the continual encouragement and accountability of the group.

I often wonder what would have happened in some of churches in which I was involved, had I had the insight to have invested myself more fully in in-depth training relationships.

When I began worshiping with one of them, I began to discover that while there were some very good people; the best description of this church I could arrive at then and now, is Corinth. Yet I remember, not long after arriving, being surprised by an individual I later discovered was struggling with immorality, when he discovered my wife and I, in the church sanctuary praying. His comment, I have not seen that in a long time. Obviously there was a longing for something more, something vital that would change his life.

At that point in my life I felt a deep need for deep Christian fellowship and support, support and fellowship that I was not getting. In part I was afraid to reveal my own struggles, because I was afraid of damaging their already weak faith.

Jesus often reached out to his disciples for fellowship and support. Clear examples are seen both at the Lord's Supper and on the Mount of Olives. Even when they obviously failed him most grievously as on the Mount of Olives; remember they went to sleep on him; still he was patient with them. I suspect that had I prayerfully been willing to expose my weakness to persons God lead me to, God could have brought a group together and developed all of us to his Glory and the reaching of others.

More recently, frustrated in my attempts to train and equip a group in lifestyle evangelism, I backed off and invited two couples to join me in a discipling group. The upfront intent was to disciple each other, to pray together, study together, reach out together. While I primarily lead the group; from the beginning the focus was on discipling each other rather than on me discipling them. Several things happened that I was not anticipating. First, we began to see doors open in the arena of our interaction with unbelievers.

About a year prior, we had deliberately accepted a position as caretakers of a therapeutic horse riding stable with about 75 handicapped riders per week, and approximately an equal number of weekly volunteers. During our time there, we had more ministry opportunities, and we saw more conversions in a short period than I had ever seen in a comparable time even when I was pastoring.

We lived on site: at one point as we were preparing to move, we literally had another person barge through the door before we wrapped up serious conversation, with the proceeding person. I really believe it was the prayers and faith of the group that opened the doors to God working in our midst in this way.

We had become tight as a group. This was not because we were exclusive. We deliberately avoided prolonged association at church, in order to greet newcomers. We regularly invited and had others attending our group meetings. We shared Thanksgiving dinner and some Sunday meals together along with invited guests, both believers and non-believers.

Second, unknown to us, others in the congregation were watching us. Finally, the pastor asked me how we had achieved such closeness. While growing rapidly, the Church at that time was struggling with the isolation of its member from each other, and the need for greater cohesiveness as a congregation. Along with other models, our group became a model, as small group ministries in the church were revamped.

2. Train in order to reproduce

Most people would assume that if you win someone to Christ, you have reproduced yourself. It seems logical. There was one, now there are two; but it just is not true. You still have not completed the process.

Biologically if you produce one more and then allow that one to starve to death, you do not have greater numbers, just more experience. Spiritually if you reproduce one more, but that one cannot reproduce, you have gained only a convert. It is not keeping the reproductive process alive.

In 2 Timothy 2:2 the apostle Paul gives clear instruction that enables us to see what really must happen. "The things you have heard me say in the presence of many witnesses entrust to reliable men who will be qualified to teach others.

To see this clearly let's assume that Paul lead Timothy to Christ and then left him to fend for himself, which is what often happens. That would probably be the end of it, because Paul has not taught him anything. Assuming that Timothy knows little or nothing as a Christian he may not survive himself, let alone win anyone else to Christ.

Now let's assume that Paul teaches Timothy how to live for Christ and how to win someone else to Christ. Paul has taken a giant step toward reproducing himself. But the task is not yet complete unless Paul goes on to teach Timothy how to teach his converts how to live for Christ, and equip them for evangelism. Not until this happens can Paul go away confident that the work will go on in his absence.

What does this have to do with groups? Let me share.

Early in 1985, I walked into a most interesting circumstance. I had completed my Master's thesis in 1983 dealing with the ministry of the laity in the social contact as it affects evangelism. Now I was being invited along with other greater Lafayette area pastors to a lay equipping seminar by one of the large Presbyterian churches in town. Of course I was interested, so I attended. I wanted to see how someone else worked out in practice the principles of lay ministry.

Over time I began to get better acquainted with the pastoral staff. When I resigned as pastor a little over a year later, we chose to begin attending this church so that I could observe there first hand. I discovered that God had been working in and through this congregation in ways that were not the expected norm.

Dr. James R. Tozer was the founding pastor, however his words spoken to me during this time; was that in spite of his background and training he "had pastored the church for years without a personal relationship with Christ". He had completed his PhD in doctrinal theology, but in a context in which "many of the person's on that seminary faculty and student body had experienced a loss of faith and did not regard the Word of Scripture as being reliable." Tozer, James R. <u>A Shared Adventure The dynamics of a Discipling Church. Css Publishing Co. 1985</u>. Lima, OH, P. 24,

At about this time he was confronted by a person of his congregation regarding the lack of vitality in the life of the congregation. It brought great agony of spirit, since his life purpose was to bring hope and faith, yet he knew his own faith lacked vitality.

Shortly after, he was approached by a business man and two Purdue science professors who asked him to join them in a small fellowship of prayer and bible study. He put them off for months because of a busy schedule but through the stress of critical responsibility in the community, he sensed their prayers and eventually joined them.

As they met together they began to experience God's power among them, and see Christ work through the pastor among others who were sick, troubled and searching. This result came, as he gathered with these three believers in supportive fellowship, with their time spent in searching the word, sharing needs, and prayer:

Dr. Tozer relates, "Suddenly I realized that I was being taught biblical truth which I should have already known and been teaching others! Two of the men teaching and encouraging me were brilliant scientist, so I respected the strength of their intellects. I had a PhD in doctrinal theology, but I did not know the bible and I needed sound biblical teaching. It was a difficult experience for me to realize my need to learn from the very people whom I thought I had been trained to teach. My own people taught and encouraged me, and still are doing it twelve years later." P.25 Ibid

Having failed at earlier attempts at small groups; he now realized that they had violated three cardinal rules for small groups; **start small, pray for guidance, and build leadership**.

Now with trial and error he started anew, first to build a group around himself and then around others. "Gradually, I learned one of the most basic principles of discipleship—prayerfully choose a few persons whom you will seek to challenge in the way of faith. We meet together regularly to build patterns of spiritual growth into our lives. I modeled, trained and encourage the practice of **six disciplines: daily prayer, daily time in the Scripture, regular fellowship, stewardship of God's gifts, helping individuals who are suffering, and witnessing to others**." P. 31 Ibid

Looking at this example we see a faithful group of men who prayerful approach the pastor. We see a pastor respond to their initiative, and to the initiative of God's Spirit working with Him. After training we see the pastor form a group of person's around himself. Then we see these person's trained to form their own groups. We see all of these groups sharing Christ along the way. This is what Paul taught Timothy. It also follows Christ's example in making disciples.

This was part of the beginning of the vibrant Church that we found when we began to attend. It had gained strength and vitality not only from the preached word, but also, and perhaps especially, from the word studied and made practical in the life of its small groups. Faith flourished as it was embodied in the lives of people touching each other and those around them, one person at a time.

This Church found a way through its small groups to nurture one another in such a way that they embodied the truth Paul taught Timothy. In small groups the strong can teach and equip the weak, but the weak can also encourage and strengthen the faith of the strong. It is never a one way street. We all need each other.

3. Multiply Groups

Most people do not seem to be able to relate continually to the large group unless they are also well connected within a small group where they know people and are known as an individual. As Churches grow there is a necessity for increasing numbers of small groups. Without this there will be huge numbers that will be lost in the shuffle, as people attend for a while even a year or two, and then leave because they cannot relate effectively to those around them.

Intimacy is lost when groups get to large. I read years ago that people will not stay in a church if there are not a least 7 persons to whom they have a strong connection. Further, people with the best of intentions, can never maintain strong connection with more than a limited number of people. Time, interest, opportunity, all conspire against unlimited intimate contact.

I recently had contact with an individual who is a mature, able leader in his large growing church. He had been the leader of a small group assigned geographically. This resulted in several leader types in the group that's size often numbered in the high teens. While full of good people the group never became close and eventually disbanded. Had they decided on goals in which these leaders could prayerfully support each other, divided into two to three small groups still within the same geographic area they might have had far greater effectiveness.

Both the need for connection and our limited ability to connect require multiplication of groups. Additionally, given our limited ability to connect it is essential that groups remain relative small to leave time and energy to interact with the unbelievers in our circle of influence. Ideally times of fun and fellowship will be structured to allow for an overlapping of the two.

Development of new leaders is required in a "go with-me" atmosphere, both so we will have new leaders but also, because new leaders are there who need to take this step for their own spiritual growth.

To facilitate in depth discipling, as new people are added, new groups are required. Discipling in – depth requires groups that are small enough to facilitate this. Jesus had 12. Interestingly he spent the most time with 3, and one person John was the closest.

These new groups usually are formed with the least disruption if they are formed as new leaders are trained who have a passion for Christ, and a love for people. Rather than splitting groups, it generally works best to allow trained individuals to leave and seek out new people who are not yet involved in a group. Advertising within the local church will identify some of these people, however person to person contact that demonstrates genuine love is the best way to draw in isolated people in our congregations.

4. Provide pastoral care

When a church reaches a large enough size, several things begin to happen if small discipling groups are not formed. One of the most significant is that adequate, pastoral care cannot be maintained.

No one individual or family, should monopolize the time of their pastor. However, no individual or family should be deprived of pastoral care, particularly in times of critical life stresses. Every individual and family over time faces the stresses of life that call for the personal attention of someone who will and can give attention to their individual and personal needs. Some issues simply cannot or should not be gone through alone.

However, a pastor or even a pastoral staff cannot care for all the pastoral needs of a large congregation. Critical needs are often not met, even as in our example of the man with the loss of a fourth wife.

Mature trained laypersons within a caring small group, can easily along with the interaction of the group, care for virtually all of the most common pastoral needs of that group! This pastoral care perhaps will be given primarily through the group leader, however, many individual not gifted with leadership ability, will render excellent care to others in their small group especially if this is modeled and they are instructed and encouraged to do so. The success of this pastoral care presupposes that there will be ongoing pastoral care and training of these group leaders.

When the pastoral load becomes too great, ministries that should take place don't. Staff can be added, however for many ministries this is not only expensive but deprives the body of Christ its opportunity to mature and flourish through ministry. Second, as isolation occurs, spiritual life will tend to stagnate or degenerate. New people are neglected and particularly introverts will have great difficulty getting acquainted.

Small groups with trained leaders who themselves have been discipled and have a pastoral heart, will naturally meet this need. Connection and unity will be maintained through regular and consistent training of small group leaders. The fellowship and encouragement of group leaders with each other will aid and assist their ministry within the group they lead.

5. Interact as the "body" in prayer ministry

Jesus said, "I tell you that if two of you on earth agree about anything you ask for, it will be done for you by my Father in heaven. For where two or three come together in my name, there I am with them." Matt. 18:19-20

These words have special significance for small groups. God's power is multiplied among us as we work and pray together. Jesus speaks of agreement about what we ask for in prayer. Complete unity of purpose, total agreement in prayer comes, as we share together with other, as we become completely united in fellowship with God, serving unswervingly under the one head of the body, Jesus Christ our Lord. This can happen in small groups, thus we become stronger. He is better able to work through us.

When he is head, when the group really seeks to allow him to be fully Lord, a new dynamic develops. When we act as lone rangers we often go on tangents that may not be of God. When a group seriously seeks God together and are willing to submit to Christ's authority, the group is more likely to come to an accurate understanding of how God wants to work, and thus how to pray. God is quite willing to grant their requests that are in line with his purpose, that His work may be accomplished through them. In this God is glorified. When He is glorified in the eyes of those whose lives you touch, He is able to draw them to Himself.

As Christ followers, we are attempting to enable others around us to come to place their faith in Jesus Christ. However, **it is only when he is lifted up among us,** when people see the glory of the only Son of God, not as the caricature of Christ that the church often presents, rather as they see him as He really is; that they are then prompted within themselves to choose to believe.

This <u>unity of purpose and agreement in prayer</u> is most likely to happen when (1) there has been the fellowship of prayer around the Word, in a small group that is committed to each other in the love that comes only from God; (2) when they have studied and sought God together and have begun to discover his purpose for them, (3) when they have discover how he wants to work around them with the persons, and in the circumstances of their community. It takes time and serious commitment to get beyond the superficial, and our own selfish interests and needs for this to happen. When it does people will know the joy of fellowship with God and with each other on the deepest level.

Prayer in small groups while ranging across the scope of the worlds needs **should be centered in the day to day needs of the group, their families, and those in their immediate circle of influence.** No one else in this world can pray for these needs as this group can. No one else will have the interest to pray, that this group does. If Bob and Ellen have just discovered that their son has gotten into the wrong crowd and gotten on drugs and is abusing alcohol, they desperately need the prayer and support of their group.

It is not just the son that need prayer, Bob and Ellen may be quite paralyzed by their fears, their sense of failure whether real or imagined; their shame and probably lack of faith. They need their group to literally bring them into the presence of Jesus. Can you as part of this group be as the men who place their paralyzed friend on a stretcher and lowered him through the roof in front of Jesus? This could be any number of circumstances, loss of job, loss of spouse, cancer, ad infinitum. What kinds of miracles does God want to produce as we pray?

We need to, where possible, to agree and pray as specifically as possible. I am impressed by the specific prayers and their answers found in Scripture. Yet most of the prayers I hear are so general that one would never know if the they are answered at all.

Rarely do I see times when believer assess the need, agree in their petition in advance, then join in prayer together for the need. Yet the scripture is clear that God grants the request of such prayers. 1 John 5:14-15 states: "This is the confidence we have in approaching God: that if we ask anything according to his will, he hears us, and we know that if he hears us—whatever we ask---we know that we have what we asked of Him".

To know that God will grant our request in prayer, it becomes necessary to know His will. This requires listening until we discern His will. I believe this happens most easily as we protect each other from shortsighted, self-centered interests. As we seek together to know and understand God will and then pray accordingly, we open ourselves to his work among us, and his granting the requests that we have made.

Prayer and the Word are inseparable if we want more than just word. As we get into the Word, our own deep spiritual needs become apparent to us. It is God's will to meet these needs. He will never give us a command, for example to avoid immorality; that he will not also give us what we need to obey. As we carefully look and listen through the word, God will guide us in the specifics of how to pray for each other, and for those around us.

We need to use caution and Godly wisdom in our conversations regarding others as we discuss how to pray, and in our prayers. **Confidential items especially must be kept in strict confidence,** but confidentiality still is not a license for gossip, or character assassination. Some secrets regarding others need to remain secrets. God help us in this area. This is not a place for judgment; rather it is a place for love.

The Prayer needs of unbelievers within the small group's circle of influence, need to be a top priority. The leader is especially responsible, but the whole group needs to be sensitive to the priority of various prayer needs. There may be times when prayer needs within the group are so urgent that priority should be given, but we need to be sensitive to what God wants.

There will be a common tendency for one individual or portion of the group to monopolize the time. Except in short term special circumstances; this should not be allowed to happen.

Rather than allowing one or more individual to monopolize, at times one on one pastoral care outside of the small group, is appropriate, as needed. The importance of this to the health of the group should be recognized by the group, such that a leader's intervention if needed is understood, and no ill feelings result. The urgency of the squeaking wheel is not always most important.

If a group becomes so wrapped up in the urgency of their own needs that they pay no attention to the needs of those God has placed around them, it may result in powerlessness in receiving answers to the prayers for their own needs. Real listening to God and what he wants at a particular time is critical in these group issues, as also in our personal prayer life.

6. Supporting each other's personal ministry

Each of us have our own primary sphere of influence, with ministry opportunities unique to us and the persons we touch. Small groups are the primary place where we can support each other in this ministry. Church congregations can create an atmosphere conducive to individual ministries. They can broadly sow information that prepares and teaches, however, by their nature as large group few if any individuals can be specifically encouraged in their unique ministries to those persons who are directly around them.

This need not be true in small groups, especially in ongoing small groups. In a small group of approximately 12 persons or less, each person can have an ongoing awareness of many of the persons in another individual's circle of influence. I can become aware of many of the prayer needs of these individual, and of the needs of group members as they minister to them. Over time I may even become acquainted with them personally. Thus we have the opportunity to pray together meaningfully not just for each other in the group, but we can pray together meaningfully for those in each other's circle of influence.

My wife Sue is an excellent active listener. She is able to show genuine interest, ask appropriate questions, give good feedback, and patiently listen, sometimes for hours. I work at listening, but I am far less patient, wanting to get on with my own agenda, whatever that might be at the moment. I cannot remember all the people that she first listened, made a friend, who then became my friend, and I was able to follow along using the gifts God has given me that are different than hers. This multiplication can be even greater within a small group.

In the small group time can be taken if needed to discuss God's leadership, timing, and wise approach in our witness to the world around us. Perhaps an individual can't figure out whether to be bold, back off and be patient, simply be a living presence, or be a vocal witness. On their own they may not know how to express love. This may be because someone is not easy to love, or it may be difficult know what a loving attitude or behavior looks like.

Their small group may be able to give Godly counsel. It may help them to understand whether the individual is responsive. It may help them understand whether this individual needs someone to show them that faith can be real. It may help them understand when individuals are experiencing real felt need, or are quite content right where they are. As we really become united as a group, our individual ministries are strengthened.

Some ministry activities are difficult or impossible to accomplish as one individual. This may be true regarding ministries to individual's within our circle of influence. These ministries may be vital as a means of demonstrating to others, the living presence of Christ to those we are ministering to.

Often the whole local church does not need to be mobilized, nor is there time. But the small group in easy contact with each other can respond quickly, efficiently, and in genuine love. For example, suppose a neighbors sewer line breaks allowing raw sewage into the basement. Perhaps the neighbor is elderly on limited income. Perhaps it is a single struggling parent. The quick loving response of small group members can build a bridge of love and communication across which perhaps at a later time the gospel can cross.

Remember Alice and Sherry? Suppose Sherry had been listening and sensitive to Alice's need for friends. Suppose she had invited her along with some of the other ladies to do what ladies enjoy doing? Suppose Sherry had deliberately canceled out on some engagements to accept Alice's invitations and made it plain that she did want to be friends? Suppose there had been plans made that included couples in a non-church activity?

7. Accountable to each other

The exact purpose of any small group may be as varied as are the persons within it. As a result the degree of accountability will also of necessity be varied, however some degree of accountability needs to be present or the group will accomplish little of lasting good.

Many people in our generation would chaff at the high level of accountability required in John Wesley's bands. The bands were made up of about 12 core persons meeting weekly to share accounts of their temptations, triumphs, and faults in the strictest confidence. Yet history records not only the vitality of these groups, and the spread of revival across Britain and America, it also credits this movement as a primary factor that changed Britain from the inside out, helping right some of the wrongs prevalent in that period of history.

This movement is likely a major factor which prevented anarchy in Britain, like that which took place in France. As persons were changed, Wesley encouraged their movement back into their society, as agents of change. Wesley encouraged social work in many varied areas, - continuous large collections for the poor, health care, ministering to the sick, loans to deserving persons; the **greatest work** however went on in an unorganized manner as people recognized need around them and often in an anonymous manner supplied the need.

As a result of the widespread behavior of the Methodist in this fashion, the fabric of society itself began to be affected. Methodist began to prosper, which gave them additional resources from which to give. Especially in the early years they gave generously. As society was effected, such problems as drunkenness were reduced, work efficiency and dependability improved.

All of this impacted people such that people turned to Christ, in such large numbers that opponents charged that people were turning to Christ, simply for the economic benefit.

In Early Methodism the societies, or local congregations in our terminology, were divided into classes generally were made of about 12 persons who met together to pray, to sing, to give, (the original purpose of the class was to receive offerings for the poor), but the central part of the meeting was the examination in which each attendee was examined one at a time by the class leader with the leader responding appropriately with rebuke, exhortation, or advice.

Lead by rich and poor: cultured and uneducated these groups numbered at least eight thousand by the end of the 19th century. It was here in the midst of this level of accountability that fellowship, faith, commitment, and joy grew. They went forth as zealous, joyous witness to demonstrate in the community the possibility of a salvation that changed their life's, to others around them.

Note: there was a clear joining of clear joyous witness with strong giving to those in need around them. Remember these groups were originally formed to raise money to give to the poor. Imagine our churches with that emphasis on giving.

This level of accountability would not generally set well in our western culture. Whoever those serious about their relationship with God, with their accountability to Him, who learn over time to trust one another, love another; could if they choose, voluntarily encourage one another toward God and His work through this type of openness with one another.

Dr James Tozer in <u>A Shared Adventure</u> discusses the pros and cons of strict rules of accountability in their small group experience. Some of their leaders, lead very successful and fruitful groups with strict accountability required for inclusion in the group. Jim (as I knew him) preferred less rigidity, he strongly encourage the groups to commit to the following commitments:

1. We will seek to grow in our relationship with Christ by making the following covenants:
    a. I will read prayerfully at least twelve verses of Scripture six days a week.
    b. I will spend at least ten minutes alone in prayer six days a week.
    c. I will encourage other members of the group in a deeper walk with Christ.

2. We will seek to grow in relationship to each other by making the following covenants:
    a. I will attend group fellowship regularly.
    b. I will share insights I have gained from my study of Scripture.

    c. I will be available to you. There is nothing you have done or will do that will make me stop loving you.

    d. I will pray for you

    e. I will try to hear and understand what you say.

    f. I will promise to keep all you share in confidence.

    g. I will seek to encourage you and support you for God's best.

    h. I will reveal my hurts, struggles, and joys so you will know how to pray for me.

    i. I will ask you to hold me accountable for realizing God's best for:
        i. My understanding of God's word
        ii. My family
        iii. My emotional healing
        iv. My commitment to high purpose and moral integrity

3. We will seek to grow in relation to Christ's mission for each of us in the world by making the following covenants:

    a. I will seek God's best for my work.

    b. I will seek to witness to others concerning my faith.

    c. As a fellowship group we will seek an outreach opportunity, perhaps adopting a needy family and with God's help restoring them to healthy, responsible living in Christ's name.

    d. I will practice proportionate giving of my time talents and treasures in promotion of Christ's cause

Small groups need to strive for an accountability level that relate to their planned longevity and purpose as a group. Balance needs to be sought that will bring unity, love, and growth as we dwell in Christ.

8. A non-threatening place for unbelievers

Not all groups are an appropriate place for unbelievers. Some by their very nature are designed for the education and growth of the believer. Christ intentionally hid material in parables so that while truth was taught, those who were not ready for it did not get it. We also should exercise this type of care in our invitations to our small group.

However, the small group itself is still an ideal time and place for introducing unbelievers to other Christians beyond you, as one individual. As you prayerfully listen to God, as your group prayerfully listens to God, times and activities can be planned to naturally include your unbelieving friends. This can be a joint activity of the whole group or activities with individuals within the group.

When you have "listened" to your friend and sense, the right time and opportunity, these activity times can be used of God to create further openness. **Listening is imperative** in these settings. Differing individuals have very different needs, wants and interests.

To invite your friend who is looking for purpose and meaning in life, who already has many friends and laughs; to an occasion that is just for laughs, may not only be pointless, it may actually be harmful. On the other hand to invite them along on a local mission where they get their hands dirty and become personally involved along with you, ministering to persons with serious physical and material need may not only fully engage them in something meaningful but also help them to see that God is very involved with hurting people.

I have taken weekend mission trips to build buildings for orphanages. Would I take an unbeliever with me on such a trip? You bet I would; if I felt in was the right time and situation.

On the other hand, there may be any or all of the following types of occasions:

Perhaps a person's only contact with Christians, has led them to believe that Christianity requires the abandonment of every joy and fun part of life. Perhaps their perception is that the only real way to enjoy life is with loosened inhibitions, and irresponsible lifestyle. This person may respond very positively to a small group outing, or fellowship time, in which the joy, peace, love, patience of those who love God is evident. This could open the window, letting the light in and reveal a whole new view of Life "in Christ".

A lonely, hurting, or needy person often will respond positively to any group of persons who surrounds them with genuine love, friendship and acceptance.

There will be times and place for introducing people in settings where all we do is have good fellowship. There are many people who desperately need to see that kind of deep friendships and the love that God can give, but we do in fact need to be carefully listening to both God and people. It is only in such listening attitude that we can recognize the opportunities God wants to use.

9. A channel for new people to be introduced to the Church community

Movement of new people can be multi-directional in relation to the church. We have a front door, and a back door. We often have trouble getting them in. Sometimes a worse problem keeping them. Regardless of the direction, small groups can be a primary key to a major problem in the church. Our back door is often as large as or larger than our front.

Most churches believe they are friendly. It is usually true that they are. It is usually just as true, or more so, that they are not. They are genuinely friendly with themselves. Most are welcoming of visitor to their meetings. Period.

Usually their friendship connections are full. The more fully they are engaged in the life of the Church and their own lives, the less likely they are to give new people more than the most casual of welcome, let alone engage them in personal friendship and meaningful personal connection.

Small groups within the church can be a major step forward in solving this dilemma. Small groups can be both the entry door through which a new person enters, as well as an alternative to the back door. If new persons are shown the doorway into a small group where they find real connections and friendship around the word, they can then be long term enthusiastic participants in the larger church.

This small group itself may be new. Depending on the persons involved it might even be made up exclusively of new persons, persons who all at that point in time are still looking for friends and relationships. It might result from some kind of call out, or from perhaps a leader who is alert to unconnected persons who are personally invited and drawn in. Both scenarios should be encouraged.

Always encouraging movement of people in the front door, we see again the natural involvement of healthy small groups. Now people are moving from the small group as a first contact into the broader church. In this instant we need not be so concerned about their acceptance. They are already in. We just broaden their relationships to God and his people.

Once your friend has gotten acquainted with members of your small group; and you are confident that they will reach out to this person if they attend church with you, an invitation to Church could be the next step you should take. Individuals come to a personal relationship with Christ in many different ways. However when the seed has been sown and is ready for harvest, the local church where the Word of God is being consistently preached is often the place where decisions are reached and faith is enjoined.

When persons come into the Church through small groups, wherein they already have a group of Christian friends encouraging and praying for them, many of the problems confronting new Christians that cause a breakdown in faith are already solved. They already have the basis for nurture that can help them grow and become mature disciples of Jesus Christ.

Some individuals will be gifted at articulating the gospel and may well see decisions prior to Church attendance. Some may have lack of knowledge, or gifts that make telling the story more difficult; however, whether before conversion or after; people to do need the church as a whole and they need the continuing support of the small group.

The Church Assembled:
Celebration and worship

It was in the 1970's probably October, I was pastoring a small church in Michigan. Given its size, general attitude, isolation from other communities of faith, I was struggling and discouraged. At about that time my wife and I attended a large ministerial convention of our denomination, in Marion, IN, where we assembled with several hundred other pastors and wives in a great worship service. Dr. Wingrove Taylor, General Superintendent of the Caribbean in the Wesleyan Church addressed the congregation, he spoke giving a thrilling message regarding Elijah and the still small voice, but what I remember most was the congregation singing with great power and enthusiasm the old hymn " A Mighty Fortress is our God". Both the song and the way the song was sung was a mighty testimony of faith and celebration, and a tremendous encouragement to my faith.

Just as I needed inspiration from the larger church, so small groups while vital are generally not healthy if in isolation from the larger community of faith. **Large groups are essential as well as small.** People need a sense of Community. They need to have a part in something that is much larger, greater than themselves.

If people are only part of a small group, they can have a feeling of isolation, weakness and failure. Large groups help them keep connected to the larger picture. While in their small group there may not be any recent victories, there may be no specific causes to celebrate God's goodness and greatness, in the larger group they can get a more complete sense of what God is doing. In this way the morale of the whole may be increased. If the local church is itself a small group, it also has this need for connection to the larger church of which it is a part. A small local Church strongly needs association with other groups, if it is to remain healthy.

If a local church is large wherein there are many small groups, within the congregation, participation in large groups assemble is still essential not only for morale, but also to the unity of the congregation as a whole.

During the last 10 year period, my wife and I have moved 3 times, first from central IN, to southern AZ, to western SD, and then back to northern IN. We have also been privileged to travel south in an RV during some cold winters. As a result of these moves and travel, we have regularly attended 4 different churches of various denominational or independent status. As we have traveled, we have also deliberately visited churches of a wide variety. This variety has been in wide ranging areas of country, with variety in size of building, size of congregation, age of congregation, age of people, theological background.

Some of what we have seen and/or experienced include the following:

In western SD we attended a mega church with excellent messages from the Word, meaningful music that thundered and vibrated in your chest. This church reaches out to unreached people. It has a strong community penetration and involvement, yet for good or bad you could get lost in the crowd and no one would know. This church was literally seeing hundreds of conversions annually. I give them very high marks, but have concern with those who have no personal contact and get lost in the crowd, then leave still searching.

In southern Georgia, we attended a very small close knit loving evangelical church with good people, good discipling, yet they appear to be isolated, an island to themselves.

In southern Louisiana is another evangelical Church. A newer congregation, racially diverse, filled the meeting room, enthusiastic, good preaching, obviously reaching and discipling people, they were very warn to strangers.

In south central Texas we attended a mainline denomination in a large building seating 800-1000. There were 40-50 elderly persons in attendance with orthodox preaching, music, liturgy, friendly people, but isolated from vitality and community.

In the Midwest we attended an evangelical church with many good families and lots of good evangelical preaching. The church was attracting families already Christian, growing rapidly in numbers. A few individuals were working to change, but in general *the church was out of touch with unbelievers and over a several year period saw no conversions.* Because they had a comfortable fellowship, and were growing rapidly through families moving to their church from other churches both within the community and from other areas, most were quite content.

Remember Joe? He is the young man who had attended church only three times in his life, was raised without a father by a mother who hated God and the church. After two days working together and serious discussions, he attended church with me at a solid evangelical mainline church. The music was relevant, spoke to the heart, though not very contemporary. The message was very clear, biblical but not aimed specifically at evangelism. He identified strongly with what he saw and heard. Combined with our discussions, on his own in my absence, he made the decision to believe, and was eager to learn and grow.

Searching for work he moved to a large city out of state. Not knowing churches or how to search for a church, he began attending a church attended by a new acquaintance. I attended once with Him and had first hand a glimpse of the church.

This was my impression. This was a large congregation in a large building, in a mainline denomination with orthodoxy. There was no specific violation of truth or churchanity. Yet there was no challenge to encourage faith, there were no personal engagement person to person, there was nothing that made God real or following him of value.

Eventually this resulting in his separation from the church, with no current evidence of an ongoing faith in Christ. Though he attended this church for months, he could not identify with the message or people, lost interest and is no longer in the church.

Based on both my personal observation and church statistics, the institutional church is often failing to be the Church. It is failing to demonstrate the life of Christ in and out of its buildings. Within it is tending to live only for itself, both in its life and its teaching. It is living to itself, training only to keep its programs and itself going. It seeks primarily to perpetuate itself and its fellowship, it does not seek to reach the community for the community's sake.

The organized church tends to love programs that make it feel like it is ministering, but avoids getting involved with anything that would demand that it really learn to love. We can love the whole world, but not the family next door. Much of the church is failing to allow Christ to live through it and demonstrate love in the community.

Even if the local church is Bible based, believing in the importance of the word; often it still is failing in the discipling process itself; there discipling is self-centered and incomplete, one centered on activities within the local church, and that fails to equip for realistic ministry through the everyday life of its members. There is little or no personal interest or contact with others beyond the circle of friends already in place. Often there is little celebration of the life of Christ.

In a majority of situations a **new church identity or DNA** needs to be established throughout both the large group assembly and small group assemblies, but it all starts with leadership. This leadership may or may not be official. The Church lead by Dr. Tozer as described earlier was first changed by the influence of unofficial leaders; it was assisted by official leadership as Dr. Tozer was transformed by the grace of God.

Local churches always have value systems whether expressed in a mission statement or simply as a way of life. Regardless of their mission statements that state otherwise, most often these value systems center around what is happening within the local church, rather than in the larger church, and through the church in the community.

Frequently the exploding calendar of the Church, crowds out meaningful activities in relational evangelism. They keep their people too busy; this busyness is especially true of those individuals most motivated and capable of ministry to those around them. In virtually all the churches, the time, energy, and vitality of the most capable individuals is consumed by the demands made by the local congregation. Who else would you tap to be on the board, or lead that important ministry?

<u>In most local churches a complete paradigm shift is required</u>. **Even those churches which give lip service to relational evangelism, rarely understand what relational evangelism is, or what it involves.** I recently was searching online, and ran on to a message posted there on relational evangelism, so I read it.

The posted message focused on 1. Being friendly to your neighbor. 2. Inviting them to church, paying attention to all the programs the church was offering so they could tailor their invitation to something of interest to the one invited.

Most of the time, these activities are probably all good, however their emphasis never once focused on making Christ attractive, available, or how to realize his life changing power. It not only minimized Christ, but made a mockery of His power in and through believers in their everyday lives.

This churches ministry emphasis was totally pastor centered, and within the confines of the building. Come on now! Many of the laypersons I know are sharp as tacks, most have abilities that at least equal their pastor, and many have abilities that go well beyond their pastors. Why not train them to be used effectively in the midst of their everyday life?

I do not belittle for a moment the value of inviting others to church. I do it all the time when I believe people are ready. There are many times in which unbelieving persons and families are open and ready to step beyond their connections with individuals. Sometimes in their desire anonymity they need larger congregation first. They are not prepared for anyone to get to close, especially a group. The ministries of the church as a whole may be exactly what they need as a next step. But let's not short change laypersons of the joy and privilege of doing what they can do better than anyone else.

When we have listened long enough to realize that an invitation is appropriate, then by all means we should invite them. When we do we should certainly be aware of the ministries of the local church which will best meet their need. When we are interacting with Christ and the unbelievers around us in a healthy manner, we will undoubtedly find many times that this will be true.

When the congregation as a whole is truly letting Christ live through them in their daily lives: even though worship ought not to be planned with evangelism as its primary focus, more evangelism will probably happen, as an overflow, than in the average congregation. New persons who are invited and begin attending will already have positive attitudes toward the gospel. They will come at least somewhat prepared to hear, understand, and believe. They will come with a friend who will help them find their way. They may also quickly bring other with them.

Purpose of large group assembly: Worship, Community, Celebrating life in Christ, Celebrating God's acts among us, and nurture.

Worship priorities

Within the context of worship, fall each of the other items listed as reasons for large group assembly. Broadly defined anything we do that shows our reverence, and that lifts up God to his rightful place in our eyes and those around us is worship.

Worship however is not experienced in the same way by everyone, nor is the human spirit stirred by the same things, prompting worship. Each of us experience life on the level of our emotions, intellect, and our will. The involvement of each of these facets of our personality is present in worship, but not at all in the same proportion. This varies with each individual. Past experience, especially childhood experience also greatly affects our experience of worship in any given circumstance, both positively and negatively.

These factors being true. I do not believe there is any one style or method of worship that has validity over another in every circumstance. I do believe however that there are some principles that are universally applicable.

1. <u>I believe a time of worship needs to as completely as possible, connect people to people, and the people to God</u>. The way this can and should happen differs from congregation to congregation. It is affected by size, by circumstances; by the leaders, by the people. It is affected by what happens before the service and what happens in it.

Within this context we can revisit the issue of assimilation of people into the fabric of a congregation. The person needing acceptance and assimilation may be simply new to your congregation, they may be a person new to faith, a seeker. While a few churches excel at assimilating people and making them a part, most do very poorly.

In 1976 we left Michigan to take a bi-centennial tour of sites along the Atlantic seaboard. We were traveling with our two children in our mid-size car, an 8x8 small nylon tent, sleeping bags, etc. We arrived in Washington D C to the rains following a hurricane on Saturday night, found a camp site. We managed to stay reasonably dry, and arrive on time for Sunday school the following morning. We were met at the door by a family named Jandick. This couple got our children to the right classes, took us with them to theirs, reassembled us for worship, took us home for the afternoon, back to church that evening, and connected us with persons and information to tour the city the following day.

True this was helped along by the fact that they found I was a Wesleyan pastor from Michigan, they were from Michigan, this was a Wesleyan church, it was raining hard, etc. They found I was a pastor, however, because they made the effort to reach out in the first place.

Contrast this however, with my experience seeking a church in one of the cities to which we moved. As I frequently do when attending a church to test attitudes, I arrived early, kept myself available, hung around after, but did not introduce myself. I did this two Sundays in a row, at the same reasonable sized evangelical church. I was never greeted, even once, by any one!

Which Church do you think helped me to be more open and responsive to worship? Had I been a person struggling with self-worth, unhealthy habits, would I even make another attempt? Anywhere?

2. <u>I believe that a church needs to have music that connects with a person on all levels: connecting to the heart, a person's emotions, their intellect, and their will.</u> I really doesn't matter the age of the music, or the style. I have seen all of it done with excellence, I have seen all of it done appallingly awful. I am not even speaking of skill. I have seen plenty of people of little talent but great love for God make a worship service come alive.

Words do matter, including the words of music. Words can be the means of communicating in music what they cannot through preaching. Words set to music can touch the heart, whether a person responds primarily as an act of the will, through their thinking process, or an emotional response. Time need to be taken to carefully select music which has the message God can use.

The style of music needs to represent both the type of persons who are currently a part of the congregation, as well as the persons whom we wish to reach. In many instances, older persons (of maturity?) ought to sacrifice to have or include styles they do not like in order to reach younger persons with the gospel.

When and if changing styles we really should know the preferences of those we wish to reach. Some seem to think that loud alone is what is required. While interim pastor of a church we attended, we had 3 families with youth begin to attend. The second Sunday of attendance I asked one of the youth how he was fitting in. His response surprised me. We had a pretty lively music program ourselves, yet he said "I like it here, it's quieter".

3. **Preaching must be both thoroughly biblical, and fully connected with life and people.** People, all people, struggle with life. Truth for life is found in the Word, Christ the Word, the written word, but it must be applied to life here and now with both Truth and Grace. To do less is both a truncation of the gospel, and a deprivation of those who seek.

The role of Preaching

Frankly most of the time, I love to preach. If my self-evaluation is anywhere close to the truth, I have been a good preacher, perhaps above average. Regardless: there are several things that are obvious.

First, no message is effective to those who are not there and do not hear the message.

Second, even if everyone of a congregation were present for every service, you cannot give everyone what they need in a few messages. In fact, the needs are so varied you will be fortunate if you even give a few what they need with a lot of messages.

Third, if evangelism is the top priority in most messages, then the ongoing process of discipleship, so essential to growth and maturity; will be neglected.

What then should be the central focus and priority of Preaching? I believe that the central focus should be making disciples. Wow! Wait a minute; I thought you said evangelism should not be the central focus of preaching in the worship service of a local Church. True, but the two are not the same.

Evangelism focuses on the decision, to begin following Christ. Making disciples includes all of the elements leading up to a decision, the decision, and all of the life changes, and disciplines, involved in dwelling in Christ, and Christ in us. It includes really learning about and from Jesus Christ. It includes all the essential element to both live and minister as a Christ follower. Within this context I believe the following themes are essential and must be constantly recurring in a variety of forms and with dominating emphasis.

Centrality of Christ in preaching

Without Christ, we do not have Christianity! Christ alive, living within, redeeming, reconciling, renewing, changing our lives from the inside out by his power through His Spirit is our only hope. It is the only hope of the world around us. Preaching must keep Christ central. Preaching must presenting Christ in such a way that people, including Christian, see that outside of knowing Christ in a vital manner, their hope is misguided They must see that outside of a vital relationship with Christ, their morality leads to legalism and a righteousness based on works; rather than a righteousness from God by and through faith.

Basic, broad, Discipleship themes

1. Knowledge of God, seen through Jesus Christ.
2. Sin and separation from God.
3. The Word of God in the life the disciple
4. Understanding man from the Word
5. Born again life
6. The Spirit in our lives
7. The greatest commandments
8. Faith
9. Prayer
10. Knowing God's will
11. Commitment
12. Obedience
13. Priorities in the Christian life
14. Worship
15. Temptation and Victory over sin.
16. Reproducing faith in others

Certainly these messages ought not to neglect the mater of helping people come to a personal choice to believe. But are any of these subjects ones wherein a choice to believe is excluded?

Preaching and/or teaching that leads toward lifestyles and words that reach people for Christ is a critical and essential challenge.

Practical, how to live a Christian lifestyle messages, that teach lifestyles that glorify Christ before neighbors.

Stories, illustrations, and ways to tell the words of the Gospel. The more people know clearly the primary issues related to the gospel and how to express these ideas to others the more comfortable they will become in doing so.

Preaching to Equip

Equipping is a word that has special meaning for me. In the 1611 King James translation of the bible the Ephesians 4 passage implies that Evangelist, pastors, and teachers were to do the work of the ministry, and so it has been largely practiced with laypersons simply becoming their assistants.

I discovered very differently when I began to explore this passage through the original Greek and newer translations in the late 70's and early 80's. It is in fact, the role of this group of specialist to prepare, or **Equip** the church for its ministry, rather than their responsibility to do the ministry.

This fact has become generally accepted in the church since that time. It has been accepted as true, it has been given lip service, but very little practiced. It is yet to be woven into the fabric of our sermon preparation, or the life and practice of our local churches.

Even as I believe that evangelism can be woven into nearly every message we preach even though it is not the dominant theme; even so I believe teaching that Equips for life and ministry can be woven into nearly every message. I believe this is a mandate for our weekly large assemblies as local Churches. While much equipping must take place in our small groups. Our larger assemblies are the beginning place and set the tone and culture for the whole congregation.

Our large weekly assembly as local Churches is the beginning place for equipping. It is the first place where people can begin to be equipped to live in a love relationship with a loving but also holy God. It is the first place where people can be equipped to live in loving relationship with each other in the Church. And finally it is the first place where people can be equipped to live, loving their neighbor as themselves, and thus allow their neighbor to begin to see God.

Large assembly times would be times when the priority of Christ's commission to reach the lost is kept in clear focus, but the activity would be to equip for ministry rather than do the ministry. Recognizing that our primary contact with unbelievers is **in the world**, evangelism itself would not be a primary reason for the assembly of a local church. However a natural result of everyone's daily interactions with unbelievers, these gatherings of the church assembled might well be times resulting in harvest of their work. Even though it was not the primary purpose to assemble, yet still actual points of decision, might well happen while in Church.

This overflow evangelism would result during these assemblies because of the weekday lives of the participants, even while not a primary emphasis. (Overflow Evangelism: Evangelism which is the overflow of the active witness of the congregation, evangelism resulting from believers interacting with those around them in their daily lives). While we would expect that evangelism would take place through the large assembly times; except for occasional times that would be planned with the congregation in advance this would not necessarily be their primary purpose.

Seeking Unity of the Church Universal: Avoidance issues

I believe that we need to avoid some emphasis within the context of the primary assembly times of the church

1. Narrow sectarian theology that is divisive to the church as a whole.
2. Controversial topics unless there is need for clarity in the midst of congregational controversy.
3. Political issues

Why?

First, these issues tend to cloud the central issues of discipleship and confuse non-believers.

Second, these issues are better taught in small group settings where discussion and clarification can take place, in a setting where people know ahead what will be discussed, and where problems can be dealt with in love and compassion.

The Church Assembled: Sent into the community

Outward focus of the church as a whole body

The collective impact of every Christ follower allowing Christ to fully live through them to touch with love those in their own sphere of influence is immense. The impact become immeasurably greater however when Christ followers immerse themselves in their communities, shoulder to shoulder with each other and with the community, to accomplish tasks that sometimes transform communities, or at the very least give hope and help to a few. However, again, these are ministry areas where it cannot and should not be a solo a ministry.

Historically the various ministries have had immense impact. Take as examples the two different areas of Education and medicine.

106 of the first 108 colleges in the US were started on the Christian faith. By the close of 1860 there were 246 colleges in America. 17 were state institutions, all most every other one was founded by a denomination or an individual who avowed a religious purpose.

Christian involvement in the medical field and its immense contribution to the building of hospitals continuously traces back through the centuries to the early church and Jesus Christ himself. In third world countries, Mission hospitals have made their way in to communities where no other Christian influence was accepted. Even in our secular US society the imprint is still clearly evident in the names of hospitals all over.

In today's secular world these institutions have very largely been taken over by those for whom Christianity either means nothing, or worse those who have their own secular humanist faith and oppose the Christian faith. Yet these ministries remain primary areas in which Christ followers can and should have major impact.

The experience of a short term mission trip to the mountains of central Mexico, demonstrates felt need. Our team included two dentist. While there we held daily clinics. In one instance and older woman walked all night to be there in the morning to have her teeth worked on.

Let's speculate. Suppose that a group of churches, or perhaps a mega-church poured money and persons into an urban ghetto, by in-mass moving to an area, procuring jobs in the local public schools, began to love both other teachers, the students, their parents. What might happen to individual students, teachers, parents, the community itself?

Let's suppose you are a part of a small local church isolated with little resources. Can you identify any areas in your community of felt need? Are any of these one's in which a few of you working together can show love and do a little. Are there any community organizations already in place where you can volunteer and add momentum and love?

Why should we be involve with ministries in our communities?

Why? Why Not? Do you love God with all your heart? Do you love your neighbor as yourself? Do you want your neighborhood to be a fine place to live? Do you pray as Jesus taught "your will be done one earth as it is in heaven"? Do you want people to see Jesus transforming life and easing pain?

I have been a student studying the question of how to help other come to a personal knowledge of God through Jesus Christ for a very long time. I have found there are no cookie cutter answers. Instead there are tough questions.

One of the toughest is the question, where is God when it hurts? My short answer is that God is right there in the middle of it trying to help. Almost all of our hurt in some way traces back to man's selfish, barbaric treatment of each other. This is true, both as a centuries old occurrence and an ongoing way of life around the world. I believe God is actively working in the lives on anyone who seeks him to redeem the circumstances and bring good while still not violating man's freedom of choice.

Some will in their pain seek God, begin to trust Him, begin to find his help. Others will curse God for allowing their pain. The response they make can be greatly influenced by their ability or lack thereof to see God through his followers around them.

My longer answer is perhaps best described using the words of writer Phillip Yancey when he answers the question, where is God when it hurts with another. "Where is the Church when it hurts?"

We are the body of Christ. We are his hands. We are his feet. We are his eyes? We are his ears? We are his Skin. **Where are we when it hurts?**

Major convicting principles for outward focus

There are major flaws in our society that result from the sinfulness of man and the US society's erosion of moral values. This has resulted in both efforts to maintain historic morals values and change society through force of law, confrontation, and condemnation.

There are times and places for some of these activities; particularly if we are fighting for justices and relief for the widows, orphans, I.E. the poor, disenfranchised, helpless. However, Christ's method was that of the Cross, the place of self-sacrifice and love. People and societies will change and can change only when by the power of the Spirit they begin to yield themselves to God and are changed from the inside out rather than attempts to change them with force from the outside in.

A primary convicting principle:

The primary place of the Church today, both corporately and individually is to be there when it hurts.

A second convicting principle is that in as much as possible and wherever possible our work with people must have a personal physical touch. **The Church must relate person to person, it must touch each person where they hurt, touching them with our love as God loves through us.**

Third while loving actions are vital, the Church must never forget that not only are we ministering to people who hurt in the here and now, but that **each person is someone who needs most of all to get to know God himself.** We can provide all the benefits in the world, but without him people remain in hurt for eternity. Hence we must keep our focus clear. We must love people in the here and now while keeping a view of eternity.

I believe only then as we live in Christ, and He lives in us will we bear fruit that will last.

Bibliography

Arn, Win and Arn, Charles. The Master's Plan for Making Disciples, How every Christian can be an effective witness through and enabling church. Pasadena, CA. Church Growth Press, 1962 Quoted Pages 116, 142, 158

Baker, Jim. I Was Wrong, Nashville, TN,: Thomas Nelson, Inc., 1996 Quoted Pages 64,112

Barcley, William, The Acts of the Apostles, Westminster; John Knox press. 1955 Quoted Page 96

Brand, Paul and Philip Yancey, Fearfully and Wonderfully Made, Grand Rapids, MI.: Zondervan Publishing House, 1980 Quoted Page 110

Carter, Charles W. The Person and Ministry of the Holy Spirit, A Wesleyan Perspective. Grand Rapids, MI: Baker Book House, 1974 Quoted Page 26

Coleman, Robert E. The Master Plan of Evangelism. Old Tappan, NJ: Fleming H. Revell Co., 1963 Quoted Page 186

Forbes, April 27, 2007 Godly Work, Quoted Page 125

Garlow, James Lester, Partners in Ministry, Laity and Pastors Working Together. Kansas City, MO, Beacon Hill Press, 1981. Quoted Pages 97, 102

Geegh, Mary, God Guides, Mission Partners India, Zeeland, MI, Quoted Page 81

Green, Michael, "Called to Serve, Ministry and Ministers in the Church." Christian Foundations, Vol. I. Philadelphia: The Westminster Press, 1964. Quoted Page 7

Graham, Billy, Quote Page 187 Source?

Hitt, Russell T. Jungle Pilot, with Epilogue by Steven F. Saint. Grand Rapids, MI. Discovery House Publishers, 1959; Updated 1997 Quoted Page 60

Hybels, Bill, Just Walk Across the Room, Grand Rapids, MI., Zondervan, 2006 Quoted Page 160

Kennedy, James O. Evangelism Explosion. Wheaton, IL. Tyndale House Publishers, 1970. Quoted Referenced Pages XVII and 95

Kung, Hans, The Church, Garden City, NY.: Image Books, 1975 Quoted Page 20

Latourette, Scot, History of Expansion of Christianity, Harper and Brothers Publishers, 1945. Quoted Page 159

Lyons, Joann, Quote from Dakota District Conference, July 2013, Rapid City, SD Fountain Springs Wesleyan Church. Quoted Page 1

McGavran, Donald A., Understanding Church Growth

McGavran, Donald A. and Hunter, George G. III. Church Growth Strategies that Work. Nashville: Abingdon, 1980 Quote Page 39, 45

Mowat, John W. The Ministry of the Laity in its Social Contact and its Effect on Evangelism, 1983, A Master's Thesis. Marion, IN. 1983 Quoted Page 116 Summarized in many other areas.

Outler, Albert. Evangelism in the Wesleyan Spirit, Evangelistic Work Publishers, Nashville, TN, 1971 Quoted P. 183

Readers Digest, Referenced and/or Quoted Page 118

Readers Digest Condensed books Quoted Page 164

Shoemaker, Sam. With the Holy Spirit and With Fire. Waco, TX. Word Books, Rep., 1960. Quoted Page 30

Stedman, Ray C., Body Life, Glendale, CA: Regal Books, 1972, Page 103

Tozer, James, A Shared Adventure: The Dynamics of a Discipling Church. Css Publishing Co. Lima, OH, 1985 Quoted Pages 192, 204

The Wesleyan Advocate, (Marion, IN.: Wesley Press Jan. 3, 1983) Quoted Page 35

Youngblood, Randy, from message Circa 2012 Thunder Mountain Community Church. Quoted Page 103

Appendix

Webs of Relationship

Most people have difficulty thinking of who the persons are in their own web of relationships or circles of influence. The following lists will assist you with this. Fill out the sheet as completely as possible, and then come back to it from time to time to add persons that God brings to your mind. Remember that each of these persons is someone for whom Christ died. You may be the only real Christian they know.

Immediate Family

_____

_____

Relatives

_____

_____

_____ School

or Business friends

_____

_____

Neighbors

_____

_____

_____ Close

personal friends

_____

_____

Hobby, Fishing, etc. Friends

_____

Newcomer to the Community

_____

Contacts in Clubs or organizations

_____

_____

Co-workers

_____

_____

_____

_____

Delivery
personnel

_____

_____

Salespersons

_____

Friends from a Former Neighborhood

_____

Family with a new baby

Personal Profile Sheet

Most of the information may already be in your mind. However it is helpful to take the time to really think about the person you are relating to. This can help you to be a better listener and assist you in praying effectively. This sheet probably should not be filled out for more than three to five persons that God has placed immediately around you. It should never be a mechanical devise, rather and awareness tool that God can use to help you keep priority's strait.

Name

Person's Knowledge of God

Person's attitude toward God

Person's felt needs

Disciple Making Sheet

Prayer focus

Friendship activities

Listening activities

Servant activities

After 12 tears of Pastoral ministry, John W. Mowat returned to school while pastoring yet another Church. He graduated Suma Cum Laude in 1983 with a Master's Degree in Christian ministries from what is now Indiana Wesleyan University.

John had one passion when he returned to school. He wanted to understand how God wanted to work with both pastors and lay persons to reach a lost world with the gospel. Thus John turned every course that he took while completing his Masters into a study of this subject; i.e. a course on the book of acts became a study of lay persons and leaders in the book of acts. This culminated in his 150 page Master's thesis; The Ministry of the Laity in its Social Contact as it Affects Evangelism. Dr. Charles Carter, his thesis adviser; author, missionary, and college professor, told him it should be published.

Circumstances, and a sense of God leading eventually thrust John back into the world as a lay person. There while pursuing a living as owner of a construction business, John related to employees, real estate personnel, home owners, bankers, sales people, tenants. John saw life. He was in people's homes, sometimes for months at a time. He was in their lives.

During this time and following, John remained active in church related activities, teaching and preaching in churches of 4 different widely varying denominational backgrounds, areas of the country and size of churches.

15 years of pastoral ministry and a Master's degree produced John's Master's thesis. Another 35 plus years of ministry both in and out the pulpit, as well as 23 with his own construction business have uniquely prepared John to write Interactive Christianity and its accompanying study guide.

Made in the USA
Las Vegas, NV
12 April 2022

47341880R10152